Repliqué Quilts

Appliqué Designs
from Favorite Photos

Chris Lynn Kirsch

Martingale™
& COMPANY

Acknowledgments

There are so many people who have helped make this book. Caryl Bryer Fallert, the artist I most admire, told me about the basic technique and then gave me permission to teach it. Thank you, Caryl. Thanks also to the many, many students who kept requesting this book, even though I knew nothing about writing a book (I went to college to study dental hygiene!), and to my friend Necia for her down-to-earth advice. Thanks to the "guinea bees" (members of my e-mail group, the "Quilty Bees") who tested my directions and made sure they worked, and to the students and friends who were so enthusiastic about sharing their work in the gallery chapter. A special thank-you must be included to Jill Repp at June Tailor, Inc., for going out of her way to help me get this project started, and to everyone at Martingale who made *Repliqué Quilts* look and sound so good! Thanks to you all.

Dedication

I would like to dedicate this book to my husband, Mike, and my son, Brad, for their love and support, and to the Lord for giving me the skills and joy I have for quilting and the opportunity to put them into words.

Credits

President: Nancy J. Martin
CEO: Daniel J. Martin
Publisher: Jane Hamada
Editorial Director: Mary V. Green
Editorial Project Manger: Tina Cook
Technical Editor: Laurie Baker
Copy Editor: Karen Koll
Design and Production Manager: Stan Green
Illustrator: Robin Strobel
Cover and Text Designer: Rohani Design
Photographer: Brent Kane

Repliqué Quilts: Appliqué Designs from Favorite Photos
© 2001 by Chris Lynn Kirsch

That Patchwork Place® is an imprint
of Martingale & Company™.

Martingale & Company
20205 144th Avenue NE
Woodinville, WA 98072-8478
www.martingale-pub.com

Mission Statement

We are dedicated to providing quality products and service by working together to inspire creativity and to enrich the lives we touch.

Printed in Hong Kong
06 05 04 03 02   8 7 6 5 4 3 2

Library of Congress Cataloging-in-Publication Data
Kirsch, Chris Lynn
     Repliqué quilts : appliqué designs from favorite
     photos / Chris Lynn Kirsch.
          p. cm.
     ISBN 1-56477-369-8
     1. Machine appliqué–Patterns. 2. Quilts. 3. Fabric pictures. 4. Photographs.

TT779 .K57 2001
746.46'041–dc21
                                                        2001034251

Contents

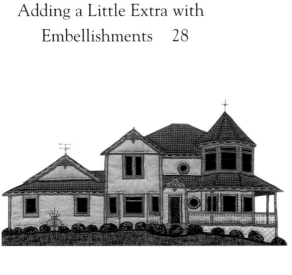

Preface

I have always been drawn to pictorial quilts, those that depict a scene and pull me in for a closer look. I am a quilter without a background in art, however, so re-creating my own images accurately and with the correct perspective proved to be a challenge.

The first pictorial quilt I made was an attempt at turning a picture in my mind into a pieced design. The technique involved many tiny templates and precision piecing, and I gave up on it after one project, even though the quilt was a ribbon winner. My next effort involved tracing parts of a picture onto fusible web, fusing the different pieces onto the appropriate fabrics, and then cutting out each piece and putting them all back together like a jigsaw puzzle. Although the quilt turned out nicely, the work was tedious, not extremely accurate, and often frustrating.

Still not willing to give up my quest for successfully turning a picture into fabric, I continued to play with other techniques. It wasn't until I was taking a string-piecing class with Caryl Bryer Fallert, however, that I became acquainted with the basic steps for repliqué. During a break in the class, Caryl mentioned a technique for appliquéing buildings accurately. In her technique, she copied a photograph and enlarged it on a copy machine, and then sewed the fabrics onto the enlargement. Making an accurate replica had suddenly become a simple task.

This newfound information lit a fire inside me. I began creating pictorial quilts of buildings as soon as I returned home. I found the technique to be somewhat tedious, but not difficult, and the accurate results were well worth the effort.

After creating about thirty house quilts, I realized the technique was too good not to share and wrote to Caryl for permission to teach others this enjoyable way to create buildings in fabric. She called me immediately and graciously said it was mine to teach. I came up with the word *repliqué* by combining *accurate replicas* with *machine appliqué*.

In the ten years since that class, I have taught repliqué for shops, colleges, and guilds throughout the Midwest. Many of my students have requested a book on the subject. So, for all of you who have struggled to re-create a photo in fabric, help is just a few pages away. My hope is that the technique of repliqué will become a tool for helping students to accomplish their own goals and to create quilts even more wonderful than I have imagined.

Introduction

Repliqué can be used to turn almost any photograph or drawing into a quilt. I have used it to create buildings, vehicles, animals, and even people.

Like any book that teaches a technique, we will start with the basics. Chapter 1 prepares you to begin the repliqué process. You will find tips on pattern making, from taking the best photo possible for re-creating images to suggestions for enlarging photos. I also discuss the fabric and sewing supplies you will need.

Chapter 2 deals with the actual repliqué process. Simple repliqué projects of a pair of scissors and a house help you learn the process before delving into the projects in chapter 3.

In chapter 3, along with some quaint and pleasant scenes, I have included projects featuring a cluster of wildflowers, a fire truck, a cat, and a hot-air balloon to demonstrate the technique's versatility. I suggest trying one of these small projects so you can get a feel for the process before venturing into your own pile of pictures.

Don't pass up the gallery in chapter 4. Here you'll see some of the finished pieces my students and I have created. In fact, you may want to visit this section before launching into the instructions so you can see how well this technique translates to all kinds of different houses (including birdhouses!) and scenery. They offer inspiration and encouragement for everyone, so stop by often as you're stitching your own pictorial replicas.

So that you can properly finish your pictorial quilt, techniques for adding borders, layering, quilting, and binding your projects can be found in chapter 5. Additional instructions for documenting the information about your quilt on a label are also included.

CHAPTER 1

 Project Preparation

As any quilter or sewer knows, there is a certain amount of preparation that has to be taken care of before the fun of putting all the pieces together can begin. With repliqué, the greatest amount of preparation is done in the pattern-making process. While it is a little more time consuming than plucking a pattern from the fabric-store drawer, the finished product will certainly be worth the effort.

Gathering supplies and selecting fabric and threads are also covered in this chapter. While you may be more familiar with these tasks, be sure to read these sections, as they offer information specific to the repliqué technique.

MAKING THE PATTERN

STEP 1: SELECT A PHOTOGRAPH

Photographs are essential to the repliqué process. Whether you are taking a new photo or working from an existing one, keep the following tips in mind.

- What you see is what you get. The view on the photo determines how the finished quilt will look.
- When taking photographs, shoot the chosen subject from a number of different angles. Straight-on pictures require less work to repliqué but also tend to have less depth and interest.

- Include the entire structure. It is difficult to fill in any portion that is missing from the picture.
- It is helpful, but not essential, to have the light source behind the camera. This makes fabric value choices easier.
- If the structure is in a wooded area, a "leafless" winter picture may make the building details easier to view. Leaves can be added later.

STEP 2: COPY AND ENLARGE THE PHOTO

Once you have selected a photo, make a photocopy of it and enlarge the photocopy to the size desired for the finished repliqué block. Consider the following when enlarging your photo.

- Black-and-white enlargements work fine as long as the detail is clear. Color enlargements are often easier to work with but are more expensive and not essential.
- Depending on the desired finished size, you may be making enlargements from copies, which can cause a loss of clarity. If the enlargement gets fuzzy or unclear as it gets larger, stop at the clearest enlargement. Follow step 3 (below) to trace the pattern through to the back of the photocopy, and then continue to enlarge the pattern to the desired size using the traced image.

STEP 3: TRACE THE BASIC PATTERN

An essential step in every project is what I call the trace through. As in paper foundation piecing, the fabrics are placed on the wrong side of the pattern and the stitching is done from the right side of the pattern. Although this may not make sense yet, what is important to note is that the drawn pattern will always be a mirror image of the finished quilt. Because most buildings would look "wrong" in reverse, it is necessary to trace the important architectural details of the photograph to the back of the copy-machine enlargement. This line drawing is what will be the pattern.

1. Place the photocopied enlargement, right side down, on a light box or other light source.
2. Use a pencil to trace the pattern through to the wrong side of the enlargement. Use a ruler to make lines as straight as possible for a more accurate finished product.
3. Trace as many details as desired. The more details drawn, the more detailed the finished piece will be.

   • Basic architectural lines, such as roofs, walls, corners, posts, railings, spindles, windows and windowpanes, doors, steps, driveways, and sidewalks, are essential.

   • Trees and landscaping elements are less critical. Trees that are visible behind the main structure add depth; trees in front of the structure that block parts of the home may be "pruned" or eliminated. And that bush which your spouse loves, but you do not, can be deleted—it's your quilt!

   • Some details do not add to the overall effect and are often best left off. Downspouts, antennae, and basketball backboards are examples.

   • To achieve good depth on an angled view of a structure with brick or siding, draw in a few "brick" or "siding" lines on the front and the side. We know these lines are even with the horizon, but the angles will be a little different because of the camera's perspective. Lining up striped or brick fabrics along these lines will keep the view true.

Original photo

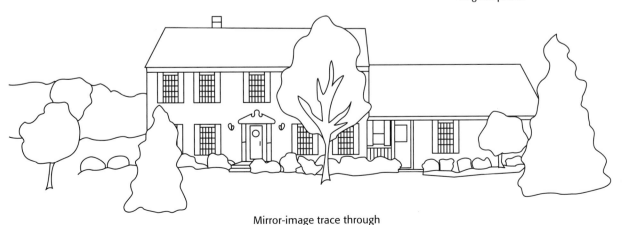

Mirror-image trace through

4. Once the drawing is finished, remove it from the light box and make sure all lines connect to something and all desired details are included. The finished quilt will only be as good as the pattern. A great advantage to using the enlargement is that the perspective is built in, so trust the picture and do not try to "straighten the driveway," for example; the angle on the picture is correct.

STEP 4: DETERMINE THE REPLIQUÉ ORDER

After you have enlarged the photograph and traced the pattern, it is time to make a list of the order in which to repliqué (see page 16 for guidance). Making this list lets you think through the process before you begin. It is like using a road map rather than just trying to find your way. I like to write the repliqué order directly on a corner of my pattern. That way, I can cross off each step as I complete it, and if it is on my pattern, it cannot disappear under a pile somewhere.

GATHERING SUPPLIES

Basic sewing supplies are all you need for the repliqué technique. You will probably have most of these items already on hand, but if not, check for them at your local sewing-machine dealer or fabric store.

- Basic sewing supplies (dressmaker's shears, straight pins, seam ripper, pencil, and so on)
- Sewing machine with zigzag stitch capabilities and adjustable stitch width and length
- Darning or free-motion presser foot. The feed dogs are disengaged when this foot is used, so you can move the fabric in all directions. Check your sewing-machine manual to see if you need a special throat plate when using the darning or free-motion foot.

Darning foot

- Appliqué or open-toe presser foot. This foot has a wide opening to accommodate a side-to-side zigzag stitch. The raised area on the bottom of the foot creates a tunnel for the stitches to pass through, and the wide opening on the toe of the foot makes the work more visible.

Groove

Appliqué foot

- Thread in a variety of colors to match fabrics and at least three empty bobbins (refer to "Selecting Fabrics and Threads" on page 9)
- Transparent tape
- Embroidery scissors with a sharp point

SELECTING FABRICS AND THREADS

I am a purist when making traditional-style quilts and use only 100 percent–cotton fabrics and threads. However, in repliqué, I find the look of a fabric more important than fiber content. Hopefully, the piece will be hung on a wall and not handled or washed. Do avoid cheap "bargain bin" threads and any fabrics that are very thin or ravel easily.

FABRICS

Choosing fabrics for your repliqué projects will be totally different than choosing fabrics for traditional quilts. Instead of selecting beautiful florals or cute prints, you will look for landscape-type fabrics. The viewer needs to see swirling skies, textured grass, mottled green leaves, shingles, and siding. Please remember this is an artistic representation and fabrics need only suggest these items; they don't have to be perfect matches. When you get to the project section, I will suggest certain fabrics, but the choice is ultimately up to you.

You will need to determine the fabric requirements for each project after you have made the pattern and determined the repliqué order. With the pattern and order in hand, you will determine the size and color needed for each pattern piece. Remember, you will cut the fabric pieces larger than their respective areas on the pattern and then trim them to the exact pattern size after straight stitching them in place, so be generous with your calculations.

Here are some thoughts to keep in mind when selecting fabrics.

- There are many architectural and landscape fabrics available now, but be cautious about scale. A fabric printed with ½" x 1" bricks could look odd on a house that is 8" x 10" in total size. A plaid or small check in appropriate colors might be a better choice.
- If there are no perfect "clapboard" stripes available in the quilt shop, try a shirting stripe. If that doesn't work, drawing stripes on the appropriate color fabric with a permanent fabric marker is perfectly acceptable.
- Skies are not always blue. Watch the sky at different times of the day and consider peach, violet, and even gray.
- Keep an open mind. For example, a floral in the right colors could be lovely as fieldstone (see "Ono Hale (Good House)" on page 60).
- Window glass usually reflects dark during daytime. Black or charcoal gray are very effective. A polished cotton or moiré adds shine to the glass.

Look for fabrics to represent architectural and landscape details.

- Darker green fabrics used for trees behind the house tend to make them fall back. Use lighter greens for trees and shrubs in the foreground. If the background is very wooded, little or no sky may show. To get a varied effect without having to add many individual trees, look for green fabrics with a variety of different leaves or light and dark green areas. Let the fabric work for you.

- To achieve depth and avoid a flat look, use a darker shade of fabric along the sides of the building or under porches. A few ways to accomplish this are as follows:

  - Check the reverse side of your fabric; it is often a shade lighter than the right side. Use the wrong side of the fabric for the main portion of the building and the right side of the fabric for the sides of the building.

  - Tea dyeing is an effective way to achieve darker shades in tan and brown fabrics. Soak the fabric in strong tea (or coffee) until you achieve the desired shade.

  - When used with white fabrics, tea-dyed or beige fabrics tend to look dirty. Use a very light gray instead.

- Laces and trims make nice "gingerbread" on fancier homes (see "Sanner Farmhouse" on page 59). Narrow satin ribbon works well as porch posts or the gutter lines along roofs.

- Fabrics do not need to be prewashed because these projects will not be washed when finished. I like to think of them more as portraits. The fabrics should, however, be ironed smooth for better overall results.

THREADS

In this type of realistic appliqué, satin stitching holds things together, but it should not be an obvious outline for each piece. You will obtain a smoother overall look when the top thread color closely matches the fabric being appliquéd. I have had good results with threads made of cotton, polyester and cotton, and rayon. Nylon or clear thread will not work, because the satin stitches must cover the appliqué raw edges and any bobbin thread that may be showing from the straight stitching preceding the satin stitching.

The bobbin thread does not need to match the top thread exactly, but it should always match the value (lightness or darkness) of the fabric being appliquéd. This prevents the bobbin thread from being noticeable through the satin stitches. Keep three bobbins on hand during the repliqué process. Wind one bobbin with a light-value thread color, such as white, off white, or even pale gray. Fill another with a medium-value thread color (steel gray is my favorite). Fill the last bobbin with a dark-value thread color, such as black, navy blue, dark brown, or forest green. Occasionally the bobbin thread needs to be an exact color to produce a desired effect, but in general, using one of the three thread values is sufficient.

CHAPTER 2

The Basic Technique

In repliqué you will place the fabrics on the back of the pattern (the side with the photocopied photograph), straight stitch the fabric to the pattern from the traced side, turn the pattern to the fabric side, trim the fabrics, and then satin stitch over the raw edges. This may sound confusing now, but it will become second nature shortly.

I recommend that everyone practice this technique on the Scissors block (page 15) first, whether you want to or not! This is the best way to get a feel for the basics. From the Scissors block, move on to the Basic House block, the next essential project. It contains more traditional architectural details and helps to present many new tips and ideas. Once the Basic House block is completed, move on to a project in chapter 3; choose any project that feels comfortable. My ultimate goal is for my readers to create a repliqué of something important to them outside of this book. Let's get started!

SETTING UP THE MACHINE

You will be using two basic types of stitches during the repliqué process—straight and satin. Straight stitching is used to establish the appliqué outline, while satin stitching is used to cover the straight stitches and the appliqué raw edges.

STRAIGHT STITCHING

Use an average stitch length of ten to twelve stitches per inch. Adjust the tension for a balanced stitch.

SATIN STITCHING

Refer to your sewing-machine manual to set up the machine for zigzag stitching. Adjust the stitch width so it is proportionate to the size of the piece being appliquéd. For example, use a narrow zigzag stitch for smaller pieces and a wider stitch for larger pieces. Adjust the stitch length so the stitches are close together to create the satin stitch. When the stitch length is set at 0, the feed dogs do not move the fabric at all. The satin-stitch setting on most machines is a range just before 0. A very short length makes the stitches very close together and gives a fine, finished look. The short length does, however, create a lot of needle holes in one area, which may weaken the base fabric. You will need to use a very short stitch length when you satin stitch details in a thread color that contrasts with the appliqué fabric (see the silver stitching on the fire truck in "Dousman Fire Truck No. 2" on page 48). Grass, leaves, bark, and so on in a landscape can look good even if you use a slightly longer stitch length. This is especially true if the thread color and fabric are closely matched. Do not adjust the top tension until you have made some test samples. If puckering occurs, loosen the tension in small increments until the stitches lie flat.

Straight stitch   Zigzag stitch   Satin stitch

STITCHING PROBLEM AREAS

Whether you're using a straight stitch or satin stitch, there are certain areas that can pose problems if you aren't familiar with some tricks of the trade. Following are some common stitching problems and solutions for stitching through them.

CURVES

Whether you're straight stitching or using a satin stitch to appliqué, stitching around curves or tight areas that require a lot of in-and-out motion can be frustrating. The easiest solution is to drop the feed dogs and use free-motion stitching to move around the problem.

During regular stitching, the feed dogs are in the up position and moving the fabric. This results in consistently spaced stitches but limits the fabric's forward and backward movement. When you stitch around a curve, puckering can result because the feed dogs, which are against the fabric and under the pattern, work against the motion. To alleviate the problem, drop the feed dogs and attach the darning foot. Now you can move the fabric in any direction you want! This does take practice, however, so let's try making a few samples on scrap fabrics first. We'll begin by straight stitching curves and then move on to satin stitching them. It may help if you draw a few circles and curved lines on a piece of paper so you can follow them. You'll need to master free-motion satin stitching, but when straight stitching, don't be concerned about being too perfect; eventually the stitches will be covered with satin stitching.

To practice free-motion straight stitching:

1. Draw circles and curved lines on a piece of paper. Layer 2 pieces of scrap fabric together, placing the right side of 1 piece against the wrong side of the other. Tape the double layer of fabric to the back of the paper, right side facing away from the paper.

2. Set up the machine for a straight stitch, and drop or cover the feed dogs (refer to your sewing-machine manual). Set the stitch length and width at 0. Stitch length is regulated by how fast you move the fabric under the needle. You need not worry about stitch width when straight stitching.

3. Press on the foot pedal and move the fabric and paper, pattern side up, under the machine along a drawn line. Try to move the fabric and needle at the same rate of speed or your stitches will be different lengths. If your stitches are too short, move the fabric more quickly than the needle speed. If your stitches are too long, move the fabric more slowly than the needle speed. Check the fabric side to see how flat the fabric remained against the pattern.

To practice free-motion satin stitching:

1. Trim the top fabric layer from the free-motion practice piece. Trim along a curved seam. Attach the darning foot to the machine.

2. Drop or cover the feed dogs and set the stitch width for a medium to narrow stitch (I like 2 on my Bernina). This is similar to free-motion quilting, except you are covering the edge of a piece of fabric, and the needle moves side to side, which takes getting used to.

3. Begin stitching along the edge of the top fabric and don't be afraid to "put the pedal to the metal." The needle will be going quite fast, but your hands will be moving the fabric slowly to allow the satin stitch to cover the appliqué edge. If you move the fabric too quickly and get a zigzag look, go back and then forward again to fill in the area (this technique can be very forgiving). With practice, curves become easy and require very little stopping and starting. When you do need to stop, do it with the needle down along the outside of an outer (convex) curve or the inside of an inner (concave) curve. This will prevent gaps in the stitching.

4. To do sharp points and inside corners, stitch to the point and then, without stopping to pivot, stitch back down the other side. This can be great fun and especially helpful when doing tree branches (refer to "Points" on page 14 for more information on stitching points). Just practice, practice, practice.

APPLIQUÉING CORNERS AND POINTS

Even larger corners and points, like those at the corners of roofs and buildings, can prove to be tricky obstacles if you've never appliquéd before. Be sure to practice stitching these examples before proceeding with the sample projects. Stitch on a scrap of fabric with paper underneath for stability.

Corners

Here are two methods for stitching inside and outside corners: overlapped and butted. Try both ways to find the method you prefer.

Inside Corners: Overlapped

Satin stitch past the corner a distance equal to the stitch width. Stop with the needle down on the *appliqué side of the stitching*, lift the presser foot, turn the piece to stitch the new edge, lower the presser foot, and continue to stitch the new side. There will be a square of overlapped stitches in the corner.

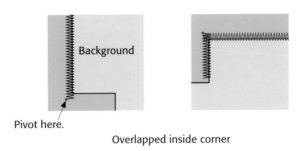

Overlapped inside corner

Inside Corners: Butted

Satin stitch past the corner a distance equal to the stitch width. Stop with the needle down on the *background side of the stitching*, lift the presser foot, and turn the piece to stitch the new edge. With the presser foot still up, manually turn the handwheel to raise the needle. Continue turning the handwheel until the needle swings to the opposite side; then slightly shift the piece and lower the needle back into the hole it just came out of. Lower the presser foot and continue to stitch. This will butt the stitching lines up at a right angle to one another and avoid the bulk of overlapped threads at the corner.

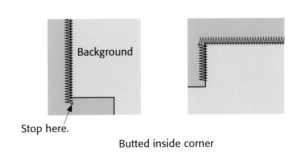

Butted inside corner

Outside Corners: Overlapped

Satin stitch to the corner and stop with the needle down on the *background side of the stitching*. Lift the presser foot, turn the piece to stitch the new edge, lower the presser foot, and continue to stitch. There will be a square of overlapped stitches in the corner.

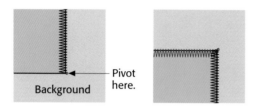

Overlapped outside corner

Outside Corners: Butted

Satin stitch to the corner and stop with the needle down on the *appliqué side of the stitching*. Lift the presser foot and turn the piece to stitch the new edge. With the presser foot still up, manually turn the handwheel to raise the needle. Continue turning the handwheel until the needle swings to the opposite side; then slightly shift the piece and lower the needle back into the hole it just came out of. Lower the presser foot and continue to stitch. This will butt the stitching lines up at a right angle to one another and avoid the bulk of overlapped threads at the corner.

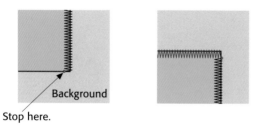

Butted outside corner

Points

Points are simply sharp corners, but it is important not to have any bulk at the tip. To achieve this, satin stitch down the first side until the needle is swinging into the background on both sides of the point (∗). With the needle down, raise the foot and pivot the piece slightly so the point is aiming toward you. Stitch, gradually decreasing the stitch width to 0 at the point. Lift the presser foot and turn the piece to stitch down the second side. Set the machine for a short, straight stitch, and stitch until you reach the ∗. Raise the needle and set the stitch width to the original satin stitch setting. Begin to stitch, being aware of the right and left needle positions. Continue satin stitching. This technique leaves no thread bulk at the point.

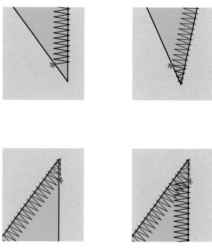

Satin-stitched points

LEARNING TO REPLIQUÉ ON SAMPLE PROJECTS

Through my teaching experiences, I have found that beginning with two sample projects spares students a lot of pressure. Why? In stitching the sample projects, the students make their beginner's mistakes on something they can throw away (or not) when they have completed it. They gain a sense of accomplishment from mastering a new technique. There's none of the guilt that can be associated with using expensive fabrics, either. Because the finished piece most likely won't be hung for public viewing, scraps work just fine! And not every quilter enjoys every technique. If the student finds repliqué is not her favorite type of stitching, she can stop without the guilt of leaving an unfinished project.

Start with the Scissors block to get a feel for the basic process, then move on to the Basic House block to learn how to deal with details you may encounter later in your own projects. I have been using this same Basic House block since I began teaching repliqué and have made very few changes, because it incorporates much of what is found on more complicated buildings.

As you stitch the samples, please note that because you are copying directly from patterns that do not need to be reversed, tracing through to the back of the copy to make a pattern (see "Step 3: Trace the Basic Pattern" on page 7) is not necessary. The photocopy is the right side of the pattern, and the back of the photocopy, which is blank, will become the side on which the fabric is placed. When you begin making patterns from your own photographs, you will need to include the tracing step in the process.

The traced side of your photocopy will then be the pattern side and the side with the copy of the original photo will be the side on which the fabric is placed.

SCISSORS

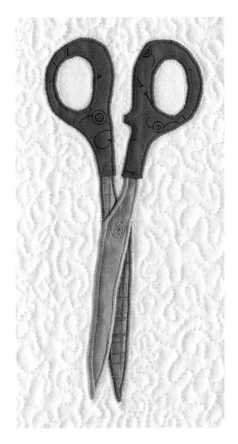

Scissors *by Chris Lynn Kirsch, 2000, Oconomowoc, Wisconsin, 11" x 16".*

Step 1: Make the Pattern

To begin, photocopy the Scissors pattern (page 16). It is not necessary to reverse the pattern by tracing it through to the back, because it does not really matter if the scissors are reversed.

Step 2: Determine the Repliqué Order

Try to imagine this picture in layers, beginning with the piece farthest from you and ending with the piece nearest to you. Sometimes this difference may be very small, but the effect of layering properly makes it worth thinking through. Each project is different and will require its own repliqué order. Below is the repliqué order for the scissors. Remember to write the repliqué order on your pattern.

1. The background is behind everything, so it must be listed first.
2. The back blade of the scissors will be added next because it looks as if it lies behind the front blade and the handles.
3. The front blade is over the back blade but under the handles.
4. Both handles can be added next.
5. The rivet is stitched last.

Step 3: Select the Fabrics

The following are the fabric colors I used, but remember, this is a sample project and you can use any fabrics you want.

Background: The background is bleached muslin.

Blades: The blades are both gray. To add depth to the finished block, I used a darker shade in back and a lighter shade in front. I was able to accomplish this by using the right and wrong sides of a medium gray fabric. I also used two shades of gray thread when satin stitching.

Handles: I cut both handles from the same red print.

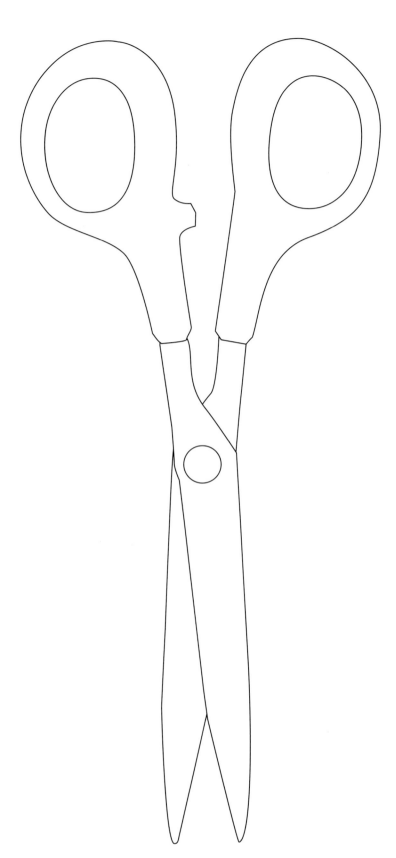

Step 4: Stitch the Fabrics in Place

1. Cut the background fabric at least 1" larger than the pattern all around. Lay the fabric on the work surface, wrong side up. Center the pattern, right side up, on the background fabric. Tape the pattern corners to the fabric with transparent tape.

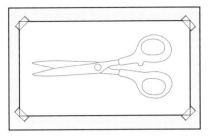

Tape paper pattern on wrong side of background fabric.

> ***Tip*** I prefer to use transparent tape rather than pins to hold things in place. This prevents me from accidentally hitting pins when stitching from the pattern side. Try to avoid taping where there will be stitching; the tape is difficult to remove from fabric once it has been stitched through.

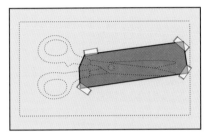

Tape blade fabric right side up on background.

2. Cut a piece of fabric for the back blade slightly larger than the area to be covered. Holding the pattern up to the light, position the blade fabric in place on the pattern wrong side, with the blade-fabric wrong side against the background-fabric right side. Be sure the entire back blade area is covered. Tape the fabric in place on the fabric side. Turn the work to the pattern side and straight stitch along all edges of the back blade, beginning and ending ¼" into the front blade. Turn the work to the fabric side and trim away the excess blade fabric close to the straight stitching.

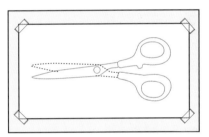

Stitch on pattern side.

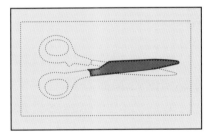

Trim close to stitching.

3. From the fabric side, satin stitch over the straight stitching. Shorten the stitch length to almost 0 and widen the stitch width to a medium setting. Begin to stitch, covering the blade fabric raw edge with one side of the satin stitch and the straight stitching with the other side of the satin stitch. If small loops of bobbin thread pop up to the top, loosen the top tension slightly. Do not satin stitch the back blade where there is no straight stitching (on the left side of the back blade, behind the front blade) or at the handle end. The front blade will cover the area along the back blade that was not straight stitched; satin stitches would add unwanted bulk. You will satin stitch the handle end when you add the handle.

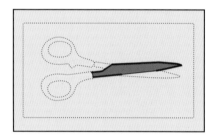

Satin stitch edge.

Tip If your satin stitching does not cover the appliqué raw edges thoroughly, a few frayed threads may stick out of your satin stitching. This is the most common initial problem with machine appliqué; an improved satin stitch comes with practice. Be sure to do the trimming step smoothly and close to the straight stitching and keep the stitch width wide enough to cover the straight stitching and raw edges. This is a good place to play with the stitch width and length.

4. Cut a piece of fabric for the front blade and tape it in place in the same manner as for the back blade. Straight stitch along all edges of the front blade from the pattern side. Turn to the fabric side and trim away the excess fabric close to the straight stitching. Satin stitch over all of the raw edges, except at the handle end.

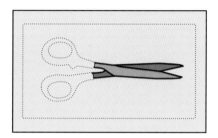

5. Cut a piece of handle fabric large enough to cover both handles and tape it in place on the fabric side. From the pattern side, straight stitch the handle outer edges and around the finger openings. Turn to the fabric side, trim away the excess fabric (including the finger openings), and satin stitch all of the raw edges. Be careful not to cut into the background fabric when you trim the finger openings.

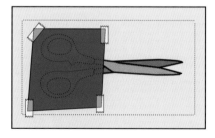

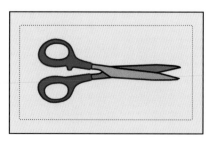

6. It is easiest to add the rivet with stitching, rather than additional fabric. To do this, use the exact color thread in the bobbin. Free-motion stitch the outline of the circle from the pattern side. Turn to the fabric side and fill in the rivet by stitching in a "spiral" pattern.

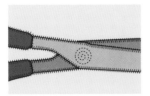

BASIC HOUSE

Step 1: Make the Pattern

Photocopy the pattern on page 21. You may enlarge the pattern if you'd like, but it is not necessary to reverse this pattern by tracing it through to the back as we learned in "Making the Pattern" (page 6), because we do not care if the house is reversed.

Step 2: Determine the Repliqué Order

1. As you may recall from making the Scissors block, the first piece applied is the part of the picture that is farthest away. We cannot get farther back than the sky, so sky will be first on our list.

2. Next, look for things coming from behind the building. This includes the tree and the grass. Because the treetop looks like it comes over the tree trunk, and the trunk is on top of the grass, the grass must be second on our list.

3. The tree trunk is next.

4. Now add the treetop to the list.

5. Once the background is complete, the insides of the windows should be stitched in place (just trust me).

6. The siding on this house and the chimney look as if they tuck under the roof, so add them to the list next. When parts of the structure do not touch and come on at the same time, the order in which the pieces are added does not matter.

7. Add the door next.

8. Add the roof.

9. The bush will be the last item on our list.

Step 3: Select the Fabrics

Fabric choices for this project, as for all the projects, are up to you. This is a wonderful block for auditioning fabrics you may be considering for your own "home" quilt.

Step 4: Stitch the Fabrics in Place

1. Cut the sky fabric at least 1" larger than the pattern all around. Lay the fabric on the work surface, wrong side up. Lay the pattern, right side up, over the fabric, positioning the pattern so the sky portion is covered and the

fabric overlaps the line where the sky and grass meet. Apply tape to the pattern upper corners on the pattern side and along the sky fabric lower edge on the fabric side.

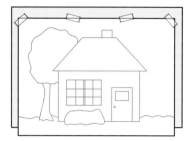

2. Cut the grass fabric at least 1" larger than the area to be covered. Lay it on the work surface, wrong side up. With the sky fabric still taped to the pattern, position the pattern over the grass fabric so the grass portion of the pattern is covered and the grass fabric is overlapping the line where sky and grass meet. Apply tape to the pattern lower corners on the pattern side, and along the grass fabric upper edge on the fabric side. Turn the work to the pattern side and straight stitch along the sky-and-grass line, stopping about 3 stitches into the house. Lift the presser foot and resume stitching about 3 stitches inside the other side of the house. Continue stitching on the sky-and-grass line.

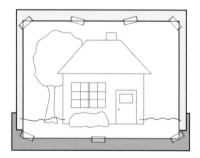

3. Working from the fabric side of the pattern and using sharp embroidery scissors, trim the grass fabric close to the stitching, trimming the area under the house even with the stitching lines.

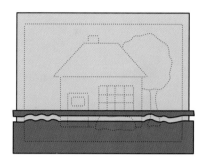

4. Satin stitch over the straight stitching. To prevent a ridge, do not satin stitch the area under the house that was not straight stitched.

5. The tree trunk is next. When I first began doing repliqué, I made "lollipop" trees (a trunk with a circle of green fabric for the treetop). They looked okay, but with time I discovered that trees with branches looked better. For ease, we will repliqué a lollipop tree here, but I will explain how to make a tree with branches later (see "Stitching Common Features into Your Projects" on page 24).

To repliqué a lollipop tree, cut a piece of trunk fabric a little larger than the trunk area. Holding the pattern up to the light, position the trunk fabric in place on the pattern wrong side, with the trunk-fabric wrong side against the sky- and grass-fabric right sides. Be sure the entire trunk area is covered. Tape the fabric in place on the fabric side. Turn the work to the pattern right side and straight stitch along all edges of the trunk. Turn the work to the fabric side and

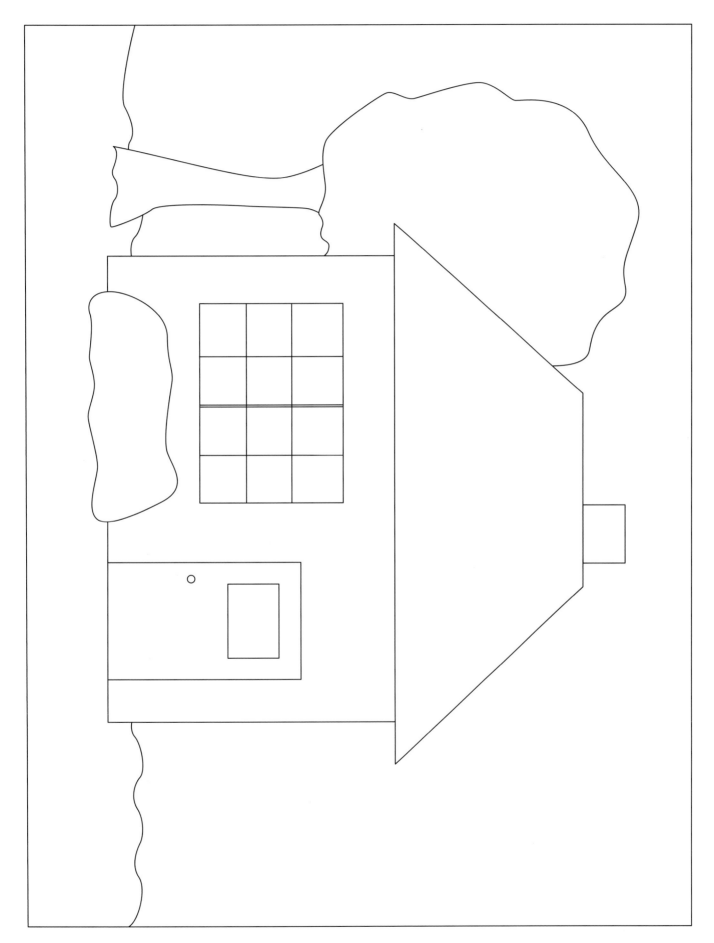

trim away the excess fabric close to the straight stitching.

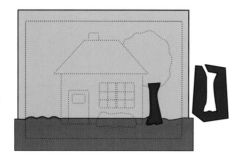

6. Working on the fabric side of the piece, satin stitch the sides and bottom edge of the trunk. It is not necessary to satin stitch the top edge because it will be under the treetop.

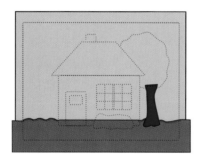

7. To add the treetop, follow the same procedure as for the trunk, with 1 exception. Because the treetop is curved, use free-motion stitching (refer to "Stitching Problem Areas" on page 12) to alleviate puckering. Begin and end stitching ¼" inside the house.

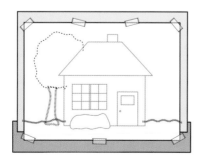

8. Working on the fabric side, trim away the excess tree fabric and satin stitch over the treetop straight stitches, leaving the area under the house unstitched.

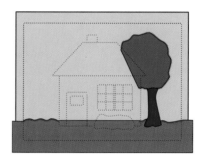

9. Putting on the window "glass" is a new step that was not a part of the previous project. Doing this now will make the layering look right later. After the house siding piece covers them, we will cut through the siding to expose them.

Cut a piece of fabric for the inside of the door and front windows, slightly larger than each window opening. Place the fabrics on the fabric side, making sure each window section is covered. Tape the fabrics in place.

10. Straight stitch just outside the door-window line to baste it in place. Using thread in the bobbin that exactly matches the fabric you will use for the front-window frame, straight stitch along the pane lines and window outer edges, stitching between the double lines at the window center.

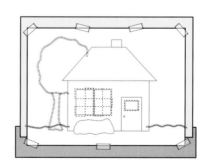

11. To thicken the center windowpane line, turn the piece to the fabric side and satin stitch over the center line with matching thread in the needle. Trim away any excess fabric around each window to avoid any shadowing through the siding later.

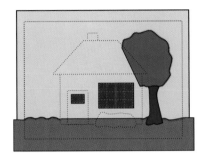

12. Cut a piece of fabric for the house siding slightly larger than the area it will cover on the pattern. Tape it in place on the fabric side and straight stitch along the sides and bottom of the house from the pattern side. It is not necessary to stitch across the top because the roof will cover it. It is not really necessary to stitch behind the bush or under the door, but these areas are quite small, and it is easier to stitch them than to skip them. Turn to the fabric side, trim away any excess fabric, and satin stitch over the straight stitches.

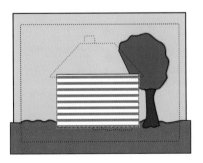

Tip When using directional fabrics, such as stripes for siding or a plaid for bricks, it is very important for the lines to remain true. To accomplish this, insert a pin through the pattern side of the piece at each end of a long line.

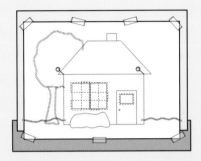

Turn to the fabric side. Take the piece of directional fabric, which has been cut larger than the actual section on the pattern, and fold down about 1/2" of the upper edge along a stripe. Align the fold with the pins and tape the fabric in place.

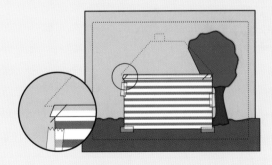

Remove the pins. Unfold the upper edge and smooth the area flat. Repin to check that the stripe is still accurate. Repliqué the fabric in place.

13. Repliqué the chimney.
14. Repliqué the door. There will be a thickness caused by satin stitches on the siding at the bottom of the door. To avoid bulk on this sample block, straight stitch the bottom of the door just above the siding satin stitching. Turn to the fabric side and trim around the door. Satin stitch as usual around the sides and top of the door and use a wider satin stitch along the bottom to cover the previous satin stitching and the bottom edge of the door.

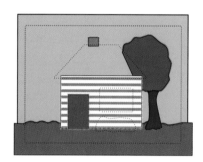

15. It is now time to reveal the windows. From the pattern side, straight stitch around the outer edge of each window.

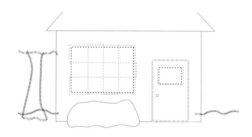

16. From the fabric side, carefully trim away the siding fabric covering the front window. Trim close to the straight stitching along the outer edge of the window, being careful not to snip into the windowpane stitching underneath. Next, trim away the fabric over the door window. The window on the door has 2 layers covering it: the door and the siding. Cut through 1 layer at a time to

avoid cutting through the inside of the window fabric.

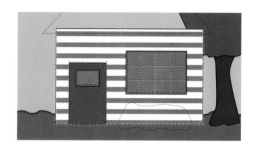

17. Satin stitch over the straight stitching from step 15, using the appropriate color thread and stitch width. Please note that the satin stitching around the front window frame is wider and a contrasting color, while the satin stitching around the door window is narrower and matches the door.

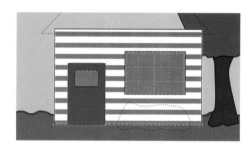

18. Referring to "Appliquéing Corners and Points" on page 13, repliqué the roof.
19. Repliqué the bush in the same manner as the treetop. Use free-motion stitching.

STITCHING COMMON FEATURES INTO YOUR PROJECTS

There are many details not included in the Basic House block that appear on more complex structures. Following are some tips for achieving great effects when adding these common features to your projects.

CURTAINS

Occasionally curtains or blinds show from the outside. They can be omitted, but often they add a pleasant touch to the finished piece. To include them, draw them in when you are doing the trace-through to reverse the picture. Repliqué them after the glass fabric has been taped in place. The windowpane lines will be stitched from the paper side after the curtains have been repliquéd. That way it will look like the curtains are behind the glass when you are looking at the house from the outside. Refer to the photo on page 28 for an example of a window with curtains.

DRIVEWAYS, PATHS, AND SIDEWALKS

These details look better if they are added *before* the grass so that the satin-stitched edge will be done in grass-color thread and look like it is growing up and over the stone or blacktop.

EVERGREEN TREES

Evergreen trees have a unique shape. While branches are seldom required in representing evergreens, the trees often look as if they are layered. To capture this detail, draw the tree as accurately as possible when doing the trace-through, tracing the color variations of each layer separately. Label each area with a *D* for dark or an *L* for light as a guide for fabric placement. This attention to detail will really make the trees look great (see below).

To stitch, repliqué the trunk first, and then the dark areas as one whole piece, followed by each individual light area. If the pattern shows snow on the branches, repliqué these areas last.

GRASS

On the Basic House block the grass looks as if it is coming from behind the house. This is not always the case. On many photographs the grass looks even with the house or there are shrubs or trees that cover the corners where grass and building meet. When this happens it is much better to repliqué the grass *after* the building is complete. Adding the grass after the building keeps it out of the way until needed.

NARROW PIECES

When you stitch the lines of the pattern and then turn the block over and trim the excess fabric, the edge that you then satin stitch is slightly outside of the original line. This means that the piece being repliquéd grows slightly. This is not a problem with large areas, such as trees, roofs, or siding, but when you add small parts, such as window frames (see "Wide Window and Door Frames" on page 28), things may become crowded. To avoid crowding, straight stitch just *inside* the original pattern line.

RAILINGS AND SPINDLES

Most railings on porches and decks can be added using only thread to create the details or with a combination of thread and repliquéd pieces where needed. Be sure the lines are all traced through from the photograph accurately.

1. Place the appropriate color thread in the bobbin and, from the pattern side, straight stitch over the lines for each spindle. To stitch in a continuous line, stitch down the first spindle, across the bottom rail, up the second spindle, down the third spindle, and so on. If there are wider spindles periodically (this is typical on decks), straight stitch up and then down on both sides of each wide spindle to mark it on the fabric side. Once all the spindles have been stitched, straight stitch along the bottom and top rails.

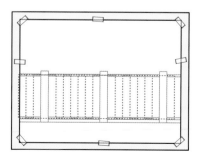

2. Turn to the fabric side and use a satin stitch to thicken any wider spindles, if necessary. Thicken the top and bottom rails with a row of satin stitching also.

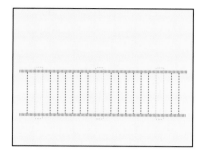

3. Posts, which are wider than the widest satin stitch, can now be repliquéd in an appropriate fabric.

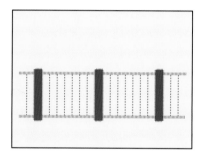

SCREENED PORCHES

If a screened porch is a focal point, you can add depth by repliquéing a few items on the porch first (window, door, a chair, and so on), and then covering this area with a sheer black fabric or tulle prior to adding the outside of the porch (see "Shady Nook" on page 68).

SPLIT-RAIL FENCES

A lovely three-dimensional effect can be obtained on split-rail fences by carefully selecting fabric and thread colors. Stitching the fence as described in the following steps adds dimension by adding light to the top and shadowing the underside.

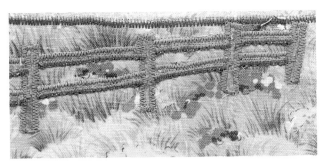

Split-rail fence

1. Choose a medium-value fabric of the appropriate color (usually brown, but may also be shades of gray on weathered fences). Select 2 thread colors, one a shade lighter than the fabric and the other a shade darker than the fabric.

2. Repliqué the fence up to the satin-stitching step.

3. Thread the machine with the lighter thread, and satin stitch along the top edges of the rails and the sides and tops of the posts.

4. Thread the machine with the darker thread and satin stitch along the bottom edges of the rails. To add even more shadow, straight stitch in a much darker shade of thread under each rail.

TREES WITH BRANCHES

Lollipop trees, like the one in our Basic House block, look fine, but what if we want better than fine? It's easy. Even if you can't see branches in your photograph, you can still draw some in.

Let's begin with the tree on the basic house project. The branches should be added when you add the tree trunk so it looks like they are coming from beneath the leaves. Here's how.

1. Draw branches on the treetop portion of the pattern. The branches should be an extension of the tree trunk, so eliminate the treetop line that crosses the trunk. Try not to draw very narrow branches, or they will be difficult to trim out later. Remember, your branches don't need to be works of art; they just need to give the illusion of branches.

2. Cut a piece of trunk fabric large enough to cover the trunk *plus* the branches. Tape the fabric in place, wrong side down, over the trunk and branch portion on the fabric side of the block. Using free-motion straight stitching (see "Curves" on page 12), stitch along the trunk lines and around the branch area as shown. You do not need to stitch exactly on the branch lines at this time, because you are only basting the fabric in place. You will stitch the branches when you add the treetop.

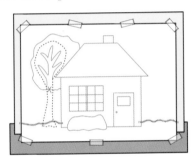

3. Trim away the trunk fabric close to the stitching.

4. Satin stitch only along the lower tree trunk and not the branches.

5. Tape the treetop fabric in place on the fabric side of the block. From the pattern side, free-motion straight stitch around the treetop and branches in 1 continuous line, beginning and ending a few stitches inside the house.

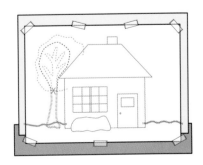

6. Trim away the treetop fabric around the outer treetop. Trim away the treetop fabric inside the branches, being careful not to cut the branch fabric.

7. Satin stitch over the treetop and branch straight stitching, using a thread color that matches the treetop. This is a great place to use free-motion satin stitching (see "Curves" on page 12).

WIDE WINDOW AND DOOR FRAMES

When some photographs are enlarged, door and window frames may become wider than the machine's widest satin stitch. When this happens, a piece of "frame" fabric must be added and satin stitched along both the outside and inside edges. Had this been the case on the Basic House block, you would have added the frame—after adding the siding and before revealing the windows—with the following repliqué technique:

1. Choose a fabric for the frame and cut it slightly larger than the frame area. Place the fabric on the fabric side of the pattern so it covers the frame.

2. From the pattern side, straight stitch just inside the inner and outer lines of the window frames so this narrow piece does not "grow."

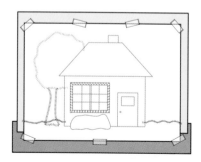

3. Turn the block to the fabric side and trim close to the stitching along the outside of the frame. Trim close to the stitching along the inside of the frame, cutting through the frame and siding layers. There should now be a frame of fabric around the windowpanes.

4. Satin stitch along the outer and inner edges of the window frame using a narrow stitch width.

A sample house with curtains, tree with branches, wide window frame, and class members' autographs

ADDING A LITTLE EXTRA WITH EMBELLISHMENTS

When you embellish your project you can let your imagination go crazy. Use beads and buttons for doorknobs, hand embroider a garden of flowers and vegetables, try some fancy machine stitches for a wrought-iron fence, or machine embroider pets, birds, or flowers onto your projects. The options are endless, but these details pull the viewer in for a closer look. For inspiration, see Kim Knoche's imaginative additions to "Shady Nook" on page 68.

CHAPTER **3**

Projects

Now that you've worked through a couple of basic projects, you should be getting a feel for how the repliqué process works. But each photograph is different and will bring new challenges. By working through some of the projects in this chapter you'll be able to gain more knowledge of the technique and become even more comfortable with the process before you start translating your own photos into fabric. I recommend doing these projects in order, if possible, as they are presented in order of difficulty. As with the sample blocks, the patterns in this chapter already have been made. All you need to do is enlarge the pattern to the desired finished size. For all of the projects, refer to "The Basic Technique" on pages 11–28 for information on positioning and stitching the fabric pieces in place.

The instructions given are for the repliquéd portion only. Because each project will vary according to the size you desire, I have not included specific information on how to complete the projects with the borders shown in the photographs. Use the photos that accompany each project for inspiration and the information in chapter 5 to turn your stitched works into finished pieces.

If you think you are ready to venture out on your own without stitching any of these projects, at least read through the instructions for each one. I guarantee you will learn something that will come in handy later.

St. Mary's
Church in Dousman

St. Mary's Church in Dousman *by Chris Lynn Kirsch, 2000, Oconomowoc, Wisconsin, 20" x 20".*

This small country church is just a mile and a half from my home. It is a quaint and lovely structure. Creating this building in repliqué will require a few more steps than the Basic House, making it a good project to start with.

Step 1: Make the Pattern

Enlarge the pattern on page 34 to the desired finished size. The numbers on the pattern are for use with step 4, number 10.

Step 2: Determine the Repliqué Order

1. Sky
2. Tree coming from behind the church
3. Insides of windows: 3 narrow vertical windows on the side of the building, 1 directly above the door, and 2 on the front-facing walls
4. Tower openings
5. Door
6. Steeple
7. All walls but the tower and short walls at corners
8. Main roof and rear roof edge
9. Reveal windows
10. Tower and short walls at corners
11. Steps
12. Wrought-iron railing
13. Grass
14. Foreground bushes and trees

Step 3: Select the Fabrics

Sky: Sky print

Insides of windows: Black solid

Door: The door is wood that has been painted red.

Steeple and tower: The tower and steeple are constructed of a grayish white stone. You will need a light- and a medium-color fabric for the front and sides of the tower and steeple. In addition, you will need a dark-color fabric for the shadowed areas in the tower doorway and window openings. If your dark-color fabric is the same black fabric you use for the windows, the steeple and tower will resemble the windows, so use a brown, deeper and darker than the roof, to create a better effect.

Front and side brick walls: You will need a light shade for the front-facing walls and a slightly darker shade for the side wall.

Roofs: The main roof is a medium-to-dark brown. The steeple roof and the roofs of the short corner walls are actually a slab of light gray concrete.

Steps: Gray

Landscaping: Select several colors of green for the trees and shrubs and a brown for the tree trunk and branches.

Step 4: Stitch the Fabrics in Place

1. Tape the sky fabric in place. Because the majority of the sky is above the trees, I positioned the sky fabric along the top of the pattern and taped 2 small pieces of sky fabric in place among the trees where needed.

2. Repliqué the tree coming from behind the building. You will need to use free-motion stitching (see "Curves" on page 12) to straight stitch around the entire tree area on the pattern and then satin stitch where the tree meets the sky. Do not satin stitch behind the building.

3. Place the inner window fabric pieces in place. Straight stitch around the outside of each of these areas. There are no window-pane lines to worry about on this building. This step does not require satin stitching.

4. Add the fabric for the tower openings in the same manner as for the insides of the windows. Again, no satin stitching is required.

5. Repliqué the front door. Satin stitch only the edge between the door and the window.

6. Begin working on the steeple by adding the inside of the arch, satin stitching only along the sky edge. Next, repliqué the side-facing steeple wall, with the satin stitching going along the short, vertical, back edge. Satin stitch around the inside of the arch. Repliqué the front-facing wall, satin stitching as shown. Now repliqué the steeple roof and satin stitch on all 4 sides. Use a wider satin stitch at the rooftop. Add a line of satin stitches in the roof-color thread to

finish off the remaining angled edge of the side-facing steeple wall.

7. Repliqué both pieces of the front-facing wall. These walls require no satin stitching. Next, add the side-facing wall in the darker shade of fabric and satin stitch between the front and side walls.

8. Repliqué the narrow strip under the slanted portion of the roof next, satin stitching along both long edges. Add the main roof, satin stitching all of the edges except the edge along the tower. Repliqué the small roof piece below the steeple; satin stitch along the top edge only.

9. Now it's time to finish the windows in the walls. We waited until now because the roof-color thread is in the machine and is the color needed for framing the windows. From the pattern side, straight stitch around the 5 windows in the brick walls. Do not stitch the door window at this time. From

the fabric side, trim the siding fabric away from inside the windows. Satin stitch around each window, leaving the edges that will be covered by trees and shrubs unstitched.

raw edges on the tower in the appropriate shade of thread. Repliqué the roofs of the short corner walls in the same fabric as the steeple roof.

10. In order to achieve the proper shading on all the different walls of the tower and the short corner walls, refer to the numbers on the pattern. Straight stitch and trim in the order numbered, but do not satin stitch yet. For pieces numbered 1, use the darkest shade of stone fabric. Cover the areas numbered 2 with the medium-color stone fabric and the areas numbered 3 with the lightest shade of stone fabric. The sides of the tower marked 2 and 3 can be 1 large piece, with the opposite-color pieces at the top of the tower cut separately. Be sure to straight stitch along the horizontal ledges to mark them for satin stitching. Cut away the fabric over the tower openings, and then satin stitch all the

11. Repliqué the steps, satin stitching along the top and side edges that lie against the building. Place a lighter gray thread in the bobbin and stitch along the horizontal "step" lines to give them dimension.

12. Place black thread in the bobbin and stitch the wrought-iron railings from the pattern side, following the instructions for "Railings and Spindles" on page 26.

13. Repliqué the grass.

14. Repliqué all of the front shrubs, using free-motion stitching (see "Curves" on page 12). Repliqué the front tree, following the instructions for "Trees with Branches" on page 27.

15. Refer to "Finishing" on pages 74–79 to complete the project.

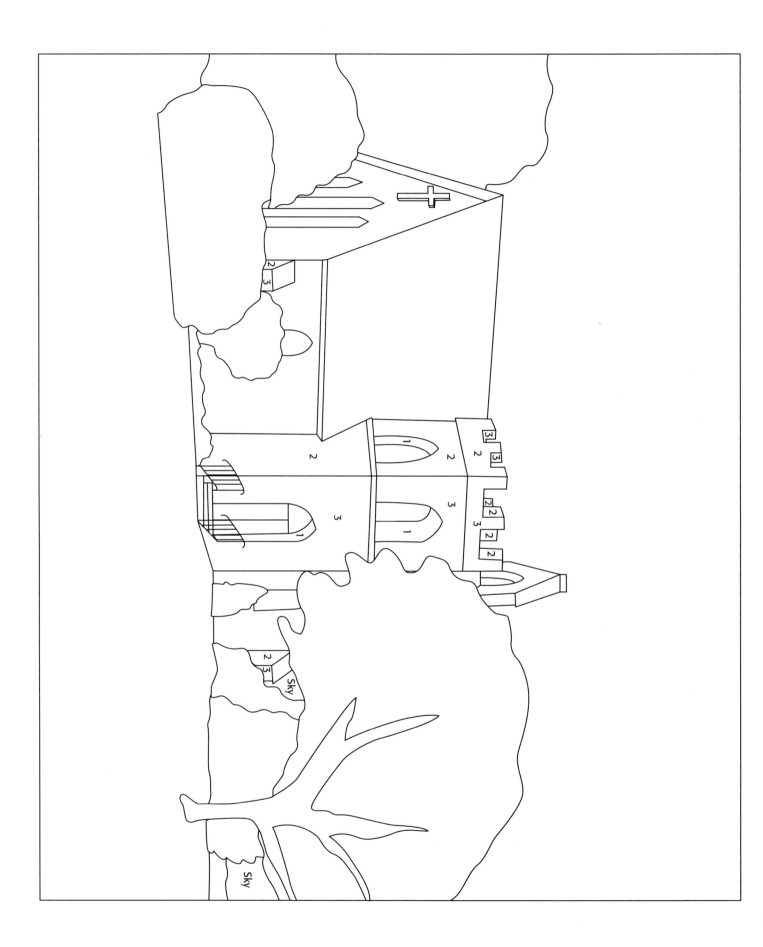

Soft Landing

SOFT LANDING *by Chris Lynn Kirsch, 2001, Oconomowoc, Wisconsin, 16" x 19".*

Step 2: Determine the Repliqué Order

1. Sky
2. Tree line
3. Grass
4. Tether lines
5. Lower blue portion of balloon
6. Teal portion of balloon
7. Orange portion of balloon
8. Red portion of balloon
9. Yellow portion of balloon
10. Purple portion of balloon
11. Upper blue portion of balloon
12. Sail
13. Birds, flame, and figures in basket
14. Basket

Step 3: Select the Fabrics

Sky: Light blue

Tree line and grass: Select a dark green fabric to represent the trees and a lighter green print for the grass.

Balloon: You will need several bright colors: blue, teal, orange, red, yellow, purple, and white. Choose solid-color fabrics or those that read as solid.

Figures in basket: Black solid

Basket: Use a small check or a print that resembles the woven pattern of a basket.

Step 4: Stitch the Fabrics in Place

1. Tape the sky fabric in place.
2. Repliqué the tree line.
3. Repliqué the grass.

Our previous home in Sun Prairie, Wisconsin, was situated on five lovely acres in the country. Early one sunny Saturday morning the kids excitedly rushed to wake me because a hot-air balloon had landed across the road from our home. They opened the curtains to show me, and the balloon just about filled the window. My husband was already outside taking pictures, and this became another repliqué quilt inspiration.

Step 1: Make the Pattern

Enlarge the pattern on page 39 to the desired finished size. The dashed lines represent stitching lines that will be added when the project is quilted.

4. Refer to "Railings and Spindles" on page 26 to stitch the tether lines. Use black thread in the bobbin and stitch from the pattern side. Be sure to take 1 or 2 stitches past the edge of the balloon and the basket so the thread ends will be secured when the subsequent pieces are added.

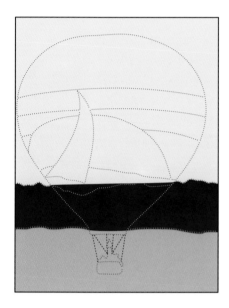

5. Repliqué the lower blue portion of the balloon. Leave the black thread in the bobbin to straight stitch the edges and the horizontal lines along the balloon opening. Use matching blue thread to satin stitch all but the top edge.

6. Repliqué the teal portion of the balloon.

Tip To keep the balloon fabrics from shadowing through the sail motif, stitch just inside the sail lines when adding each of the pieces that will be behind it. Trim the pieces away. I was not worried about the sky fabric shadowing through, but if you are concerned about it, you may remove it through the opening left after the other fabrics have been trimmed.

7. Repliqué the orange portion of the balloon.

8. Repliqué the red portion of the balloon.

9. Repliqué the yellow portion of the balloon.

10. Repliqué the purple portion of the balloon.

11. Repliqué the upper blue portion of the balloon.

12. Repliqué the sail. As an extra precaution against shadowing, I used a double layer of white fabric for the sail and treated the layers as 1 when stitching.

13. Using black thread in the bobbin, free-motion straight stitch the bird outlines from the pattern side.

14. From the fabric side, fill in the bird outlines with free-motion satin stitching.

15. Using red thread in the bobbin, outline the flame from the pattern side. Using red in the top, fill in the flame from the fabric side.

16. Repliqué the figures in the basket.

17. Repliqué the basket.

18. Using water-soluble thread in the top and bobbin, mark the balloon quilting lines by stitching from the pattern side along the vertical dashed lines on the patterns.

19. Refer to "Finishing" on pages 74–79 to border, layer, and quilt the project as desired. After the quilting has been done, stitch over the water-soluble thread lines with nylon thread. Bind the outer edges, and then rinse the quilt in tepid water to dissolve the water-soluble thread. Lay the quilt flat to dry.

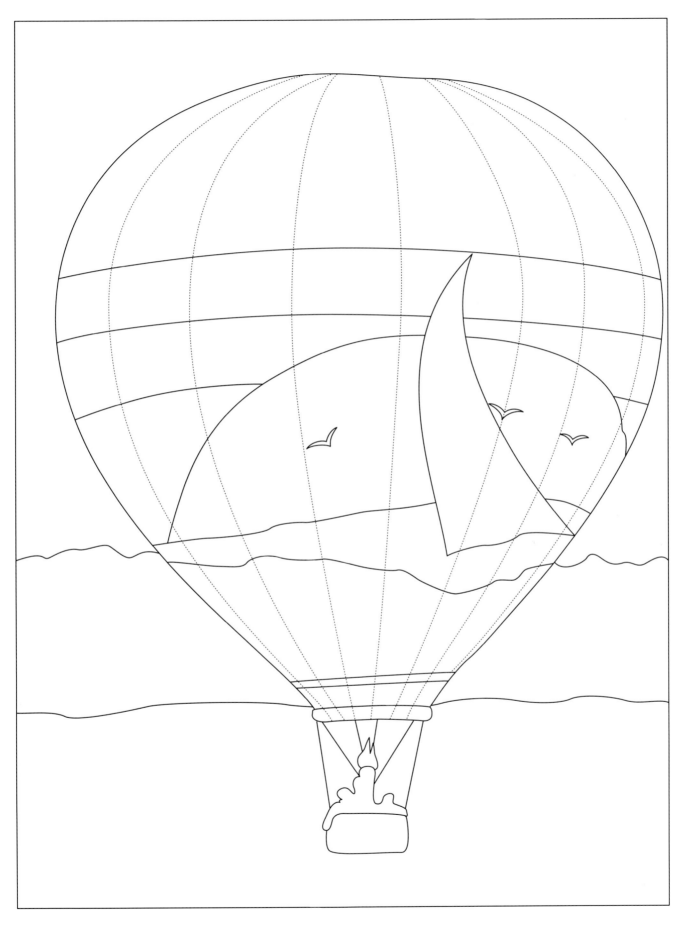

Purple Coneflowers

PURPLE CONEFLOWERS *by Chris Lynn Kirsch, 2000, Oconomowoc, Wisconsin, 19″ x 18″.*

Step 2: Determine the Repliqué Order

1. Sky
2. Leaves on tallest flower and stem on shortest flower
3. Dark petals
4. Stems on both of the taller flowers
5. Light petals
6. Flower centers

Step 3: Select the Fabrics

Sky: A rich, summer-sky blue

Leaves and stems: I used 2 different green prints, but this is not essential. Making the stem of the shortest flower lighter than the leaves and stems of the 2 taller flowers adds to the illusion of depth.

Dark petals: Deep purple

Light petals: I used a medium pink stripe to add texture, but it made adding the petals more work because I had to add the petals 1 or 2 at a time to keep the stripe in the right direction. Using a pale pink or purple non-directional print will allow you to use 1 piece of fabric for the light petals on each flower.

Flower centers: Dark gold

I took this photograph in my backyard wildflower prairie. I chose to trace the design through to the back of my original enlargement, not because I cared if the picture was reversed but because I felt a line drawing would be easier to follow and I wanted to leave some of the flowers off my pattern. I labeled the petals *L* for light and *D* for dark to avoid confusion while stitching.

Step 1: Make the Pattern

Enlarge the pattern on page 43 to the desired finished size.

Step 4: Stitch the Fabrics in Place

There are very few straight lines in this project, so I recommend free-motion stitching for the entire project (see "Curves" on page 12).

1. Tape the sky fabric in place.
2. Cut a piece of fabric large enough to cover both leaves on the tallest flower. Repliqué the leaves, but do not satin stitch the area that will be covered by the stem. Repliqué the stem on the shortest flower. Do not satin stitch the top and bottom ends of the stem.
3. Cut the fabric pieces for the dark petals large enough to cover the entire dark-petal area on each flower. Repliqué all of the dark petals. Satin stitch only along the lower edges that will not be covered by the light petals.

4. Repliqué the remaining stems. Do not satin stitch the stem top and bottom ends.
5. Repliqué the light petals. Satin stitch between the petals but not under the flower center.
6. Repliqué the flower centers, satin stitching the edges only if you will not be adding the thread "spikes" to the flowers. If you will be adding the thread spikes to the centers, use a variegated metallic thread to add free-motion spikes to the centers, working from the center out.

7. Refer to "Finishing" on pages 74–79 to complete the project.

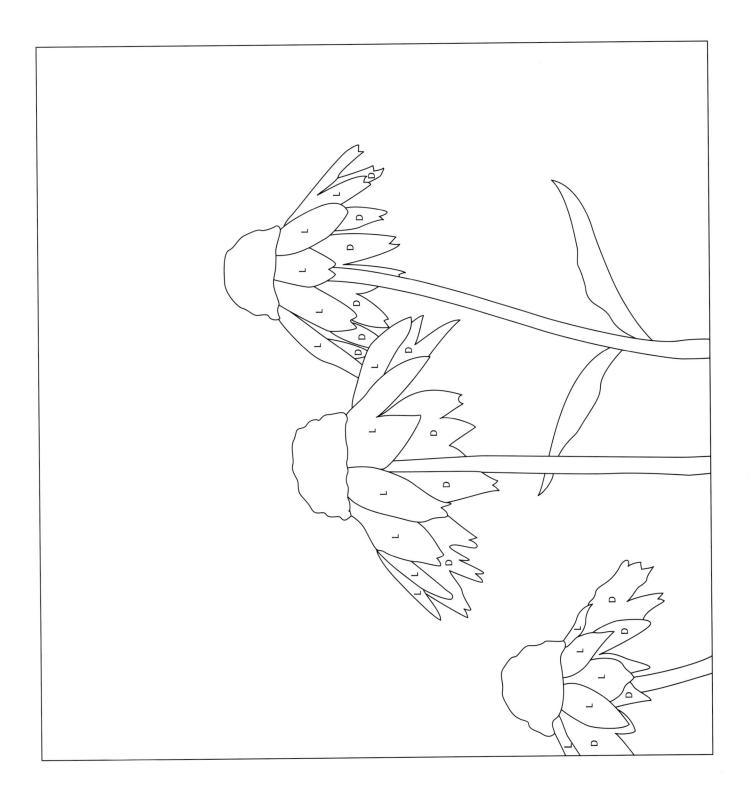

A Covered Bridge

A COVERED BRIDGE *by Chris Lynn Kirsch, 2000, Oconomowoc, Wisconsin, 21" x 15".*

On a visit to see my husband's family, we took a side trip to Winterset, Iowa. This is where the covered bridges of Madison County are located. It was a lovely day and a lovely ride. The first bridge we came upon was the St. Charles, "Gateway to the Bridges." It was so picturesque that we had to take a photograph so I could repliqué a quilt block.

Step 1: Make the Pattern

Enlarge the pattern on page 47 to the desired finished size. I chose to number and letter the parts of this pattern because there were so many trees and bushes to keep straight. Numbers on the pattern correspond to the step number in the stitching directions. If a letter follows the number, stitch the pieces in alphabetical order.

Step 2: Determine the Repliqué Order

1. Sky
2. Background trees (2A–2F)
3 Shadowed inside wall and dark area under the bridge
4. Lighter inside wall
5. Horizontal bridge support
6. Bridge floor
7. Side of bridge

8. Gable, railing, and trim at bridge opening
9. Roof
10. Foreground bushes (10A–10C)
11. Tall grass
12. Mowed grass
13. Foreground trees (13A–13D)

Step 3: Select the Fabrics

Sky: The photo shows an overcast day, but you can choose what kind of day you want it to be with your choice of blue or gray fabric.

Trees and shrubs: Use a variety of green fabrics to add interest.

Inside walls: You will need 2 shades of gray, 1 darker than the other to represent the shadowed area.

Dark area under bridge: Black solid
Bridge supports: White solid
Bridge floor: Black solid
Side of bridge: Select a red print with a textured look or a red stripe.

Gable, railing, and trim: White solid
Roof: You can use any roof-look print

Step 4: Stitch the Fabrics in Place

1. Tape the sky fabric in place.
2. Repliqué the background trees in order from 2A to 2D. As you make each addition, remember to satin stitch only edges that will not be covered by subsequent pieces.
3. Add the dark areas under the bridge (don't forget the small one near the front) and the shadowed inside wall. You do not need to satin stitch, because all of the edges will be covered.

4. Repliqué the lighter inside wall, satin stitching only between the 2 inside walls.

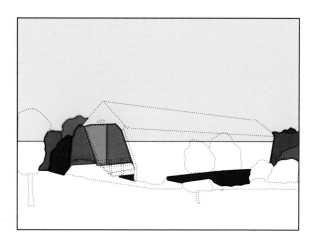

5. Repliqué the horizontal support beam near the opening, satin stitching along the bottom edge.
6. Repliqué the bridge floor, satin stitching along the bottom edge.
7. Repliqué the side of the bridge. The boards are vertical, so if you are using a stripe fabric, line it up accordingly. Satin stitch along the back edge and along the darkness under the bridge.

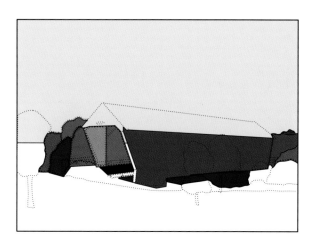

8. Repliqué the gable and the trim around the opening. Now add the railing. There are 2 options for adding the railing. You can use narrow pieces of fabric (see "Narrow Pieces" on page 26) or thread (see "Railings and Spindles" on page 26). Add the small fence at the rear of the bridge using the "Railings and Spindles" method.
9. Repliqué the roof. After satin stitching the roof edges, straight stitch close to the gable satin stitching on the edge closest to the sky. Use gray thread to create the illusion of the rear roof shingles. Stitch a row of satin stitches on the front of the gable for the plaque.

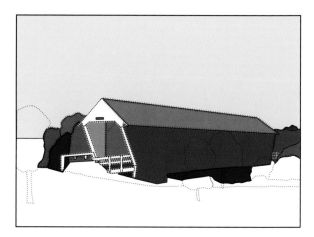

10. Repliqué the foreground bushes in order from 10A to 10C.
11. Repliqué the tall grass.
12. Repliqué the mowed grass.
13. Repliqué the tree trunks, followed by the treetops, in order from 13A through 13D. Use the "lollipop tree" technique that was used in the Basic House block on page 19 to create the treetops.
14. Refer to "Finishing" on pages 74–79 to complete the project.

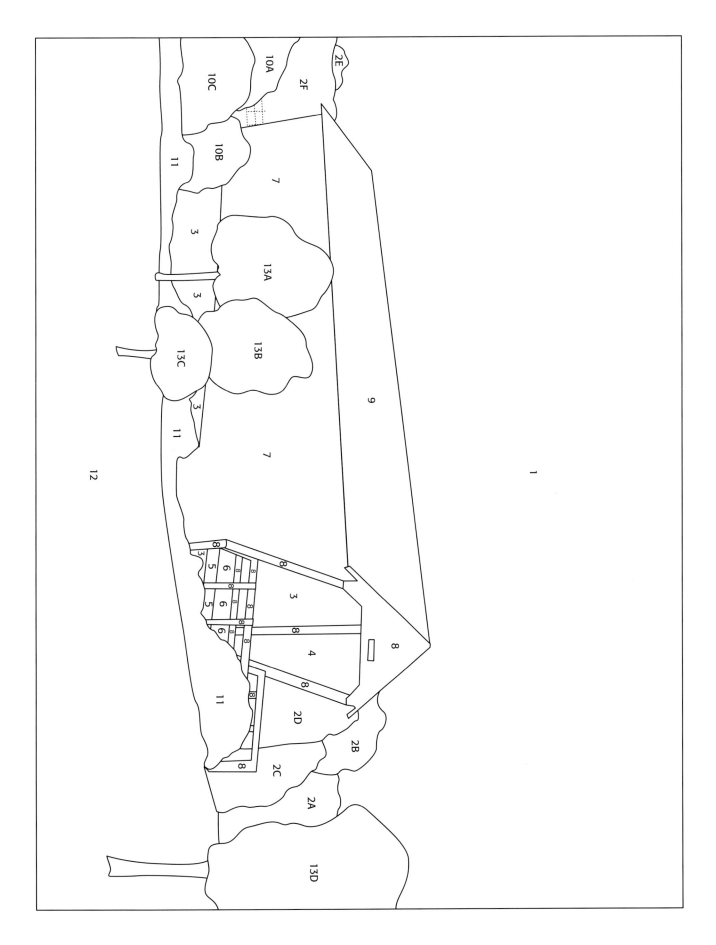

DOUSMAN FIRE TRUCK NO. 2 *by Chris Lynn Kirsch, 2000, Oconomowoc, Wisconsin, 20″ x 18″.*

My husband, Mike, is a volunteer firefighter in Dousman, Wisconsin. Each year our community has a celebration called Derby Days, and what small-town celebration would be complete without a parade? All the fire trucks are washed and polished for the big event, including the local favorite, old No. 2, the antique engine. Mike has had the pleasure of driving it in the parade, and I felt it would be a fun project for this book.

Step 1: Make the Pattern

Enlarge the pattern on page 51 to the desired finished size.

Step 2: Determine the Repliqué Order

1. Background trees
2. Concrete
3. Shadow under truck
4. Far tires and wheel wells and treads on near tires
5. Near tires
6. Insides of windows
7. Rails, back rail lights, flasher, and left front side light
8. Truck body
9. Running board
10. Headlights and hose

Step 3: Select the Fabrics

Trees: A wooded print solved the problem of creating so many trees and eliminated the need for a sky fabric as well.

Concrete: Choose a light gray print with a small pattern that gives a concrete-like texture.

Shadow: Select a gray fabric that is darker than the concrete fabric.

Tires: Use a dark shade of black for the distant tires and the wheel wells and treads on the near tires. Use a lighter shade of black for the walls of the near tires. You will also need a solid red fabric for the hubcaps and a light gray solid for the hubcap centers.

Windows: A shiny tan here will keep the window from looking like the metal parts of the fire truck and add the illusion of reflecting light.

Flasher: Use a scrap of the red truck-body fabric.

Truck body: Nothing but fire-engine red will do here.

Running board: Use the same light gray as you used for the hubcap centers.

Headlights: White solid

Hose: Tan

Step 4: Stitch the Fabrics in Place

1. Tape the background fabric in place.
2. Repliqué the concrete in the same manner you stitched the grass to the Basic House block (see page 19).
3. Repliqué the shadow under the truck.
4. Repliqué the far tires and the wheel wells and treads on the near tires.

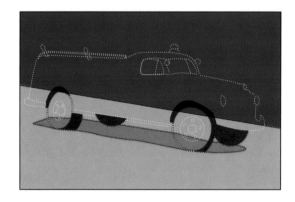

5. Cut a circle of fabric for each near tire wall and repliqué each in place. Satin stitch all around the outside edge. Cut a circle of red fabric for each hubcap. Straight stitch the red fabric in place around the hubcaps and dark openings. Turn to the fabric side and trim the red fabric away over each dark

opening to reveal the black. Satin stitch the dark openings with black thread and the outer edge of the hubcaps with a silver gray thread. Repliqué the hubcap centers.

> *Tip* When dealing with small circles, I find it helpful to straight stitch (see "Curves" on page 12) and satin stitch with the feed dogs up, pivoting often with the needle down on the outside of the circle. When using a contrasting thread for the satin stitch, shorten the stitch length so the fabric does not show between the stitches. A second layer of satin stitches on top of the first yields a nice effect.

6. Straight stitch the window fabric in place. Satin stitch the window detail lines as shown, using silver gray thread for the front window and red thread for the right side window.

7. Refer to "Railings and Spindles" on page 26 to add the rails with silver gray thread. Repliqué the flasher dome in place, and then add a row of wide, silver gray satin stitching along the bottom edge of the dome to form the collar. From the pattern side, straight stitch on the lines indicated for the rail lights and the left front side light. Turn to the fabric side and use silver gray thread to fill in the marked areas with satin stitching.

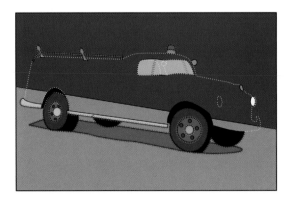

8. Repliqué the truck body, being sure to straight stitch on all of the truck detail lines (grill, hood, door, and around the windows) to mark them on the fabric side. Reveal the windows. Satin stitch all but the truck bottom edge, which will be covered by the running board.

> *Tip* When satin stitching the truck outer edge and the body lines, change the value of the red thread used (lighter along prominent edges, darker along side and shaded lines) to yield a three-dimensional effect.

9. Repliqué the running board.

10. Add the finishing details. Satin stitch the grill lines with black thread. Refer to "Railings and Spindles" on page 26 to satin stitch the ladder. Repliqué the headlights in white fabric, satin stitching the fronts with white thread and the backs with silver gray thread. Repliqué the coiled hose, satin stitching the outer edges and straight stitching the circular details. Satin stitch the remaining small details (ax, door handle, hose nozzle, and so on). Add the gold pinstripe by straight stitching from the fabric side along the appropriate satin stitching. Free-motion machine embroider or hand stitch the lettering and number 2.

11. Refer to "Finishing" on pages 74–79 to complete the project.

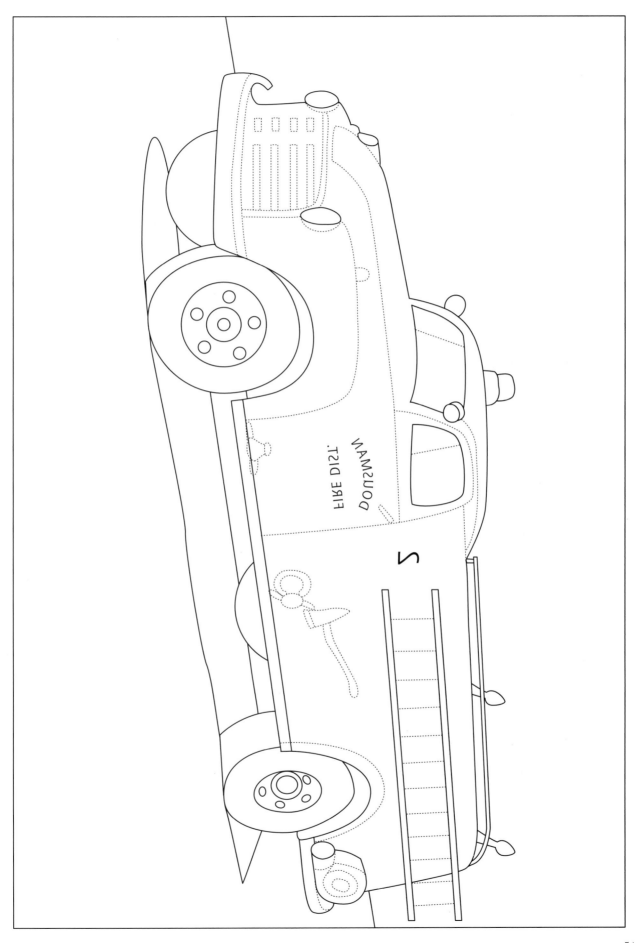

Bijou

BIJOU *by Chris Lynn Kirsch, 2001, Oconomowoc, Wisconsin, 15" x 19".*

Step 3: Select the Fabrics

Eyes: You will need a very dark brown for the base, green for the iris, black for the pupil, and a blue gray for the highlight.

Fur: Hand-dyed fabrics work particularly well for fur as they offer realistic color variances. Avoid using an even-stripe fabric. Fur is not even and the use of a stripe tends to give an unrealistic look. I used 7 different fabrics for the fur, ranging from almost white through dark brown. They are labeled on the pattern using the following abbreviations: light gray (G), very light off-white (VL), light off-white (L), medium cream (M), light brown (LB), brown (B), dark brown (DB).

Background: Choose a fabric that sets off the cat. I selected a green fabric with a lacy print that looks like curtains.

Collar: Any color will do, but be sure to select one that stands out from the fur.

Nose: Pink

Bijou is a beautiful calico cat that belongs to my friend, Jill Koeppel, and her family. This picture seemed to deserve to be made into a fabric portrait.

Step 1: Make the Pattern

Enlarge the pattern on page 57 to the desired finished size. I numbered the pattern in order of layering and labeled it with the letters that correspond to the appropriate fabrics. If you decide to stitch a fabric portrait of your own pet, the number of different fabrics and the areas drawn from the picture are up to you, but it is best not to overthink the tracing and include too much detail.

Step 2: Determine the Repliqué Order

Repliqué the pieces in the order indicated on the pattern.

Step 4: Stitch the Fabrics in Place

An image of this type has no straight lines and so the stitching, straight and satin, works best if done free motion (see "Curves" on page 12). Varying the value of the fabrics and the threads helps add to the realistic effect and gives the finished piece a "paint-by-numbers" look. "Bijou" is certainly not recommended as a first project, but the fuzziness of the cat does allow for imperfect and fuzzy satin stitching. The only areas that require even and smooth stitching are the eyes, but even they are curved and easiest to do carefully with free-motion stitching.

1. The eyes are made up of 4 layers. Begin by straight stitching the very dark brown fabric in place. Trim away the excess, but do not satin stitch. Repliqué the green iris in place next, satin stitching around the outer edges. Repliqué the black pupil and then the highlight, satin stitching around each.

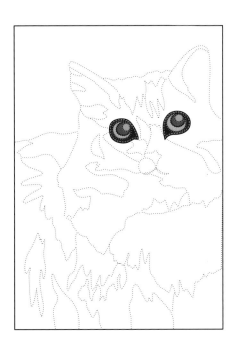

2. Straight stitch the two #2 pieces in place. Trim away the excess, but do not satin stitch them.

3. Repliqué the two #3 pieces in place. For these pieces and all the remaining pieces, remember to satin stitch only where the fabric covers a previous piece.

4. Repliqué the five #4 pieces in place.

5. Straight stitch the background fabric in place.
6. Repliqué piece #6.

7. Repliqué the collar, piece #7.

8. Repliqué the two #8 pieces. Straight stitch along the dashed lines on the piece below the mouth. Satin stitch over the dashed lines to give a layered look.

9. Repliqué piece #9.
10. Repliqué piece #10.

11. Repliqué the four #11 pieces.

12. Repliqué the five #12 pieces.

13. Straight stitch the nose, piece #13, in place. Trim away the excess, but do not satin stitch it.

14. Cut a piece of fabric large enough to cover both of the #14 areas. Repliqué in place, satin stitching in the usual manner except around the nose. Satin stitch across the top of the nose with light off-white thread to give the illusion of fur growing up to the nose. Narrowly satin stitch the sides of the nose with light brown thread, widening the stitch width in the center of each side to give the appearance of nostrils.

15. Stitch the mouth with light off-white thread in the top and bobbin. Straight stitch the mouth from the pattern side. Turn to the fabric side and hold the project so it is facing you. Set the machine for a narrow satin stitch. Begin stitching at the bottom tip of the nose and follow the mouth line along 1 side *without turning the project*. Stitch back up the mouth line and repeat for the other side of the mouth. Using light brown thread in the top and bobbin, straight stitch from the fabric side along the entire bottom edge of the mouth for the shadow.

16. With light off-white thread in the top and light brown thread in the bobbin, straight stitch the whisker lines from the pattern side. Turn to the fabric side and stitch slightly off the darker lines.

17. Refer to "Finishing" on pages 74–79 to complete the project.

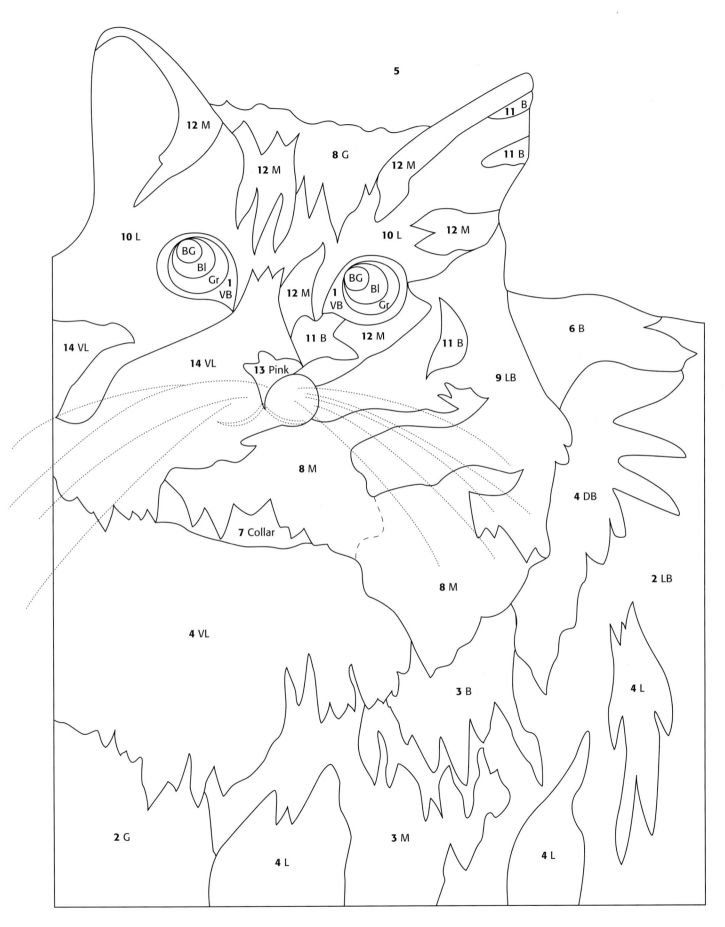

CHAPTER 4

Gallery

My Home *by Chris Lynn Kirsch, 1994, Oconomowoc, Wisconsin, 25" x 18".*

Your photographs and imagination will be the inspiration for your own projects, but it's always fun and exciting to see what other people have created using the repliqué technique. This chapter includes some of my own pieces as well as quilts made by students who have taken my workshops. While the majority of these quilts are houses, I think it's interesting to see how each individual chooses to represent the details.

Happy Birthday, Bill *by Shirley Gylleck, 1998, Genoa, Illinois, 18" x 13".*

Sanner Farmhouse *by Audrey Sanner, 1998, Decatur, Illinois, 40" x 22".*

This quilt was repliquéd from a 1913 photograph of Audrey's husband's family farm in Shelby County, Illinois. Her label relates the home's history, including who built it in 1890, the names of the people in the original photograph, and the fact that the home was destroyed by fire in 1960. The figures were hand painted and then appliquéd. Note the lovely gingerbread on the home.

ONO HALE (GOOD HOUSE) *by Pearl Mary Goetsch, 1996, Sullivan, Wisconsin, 18″ x 14″.*

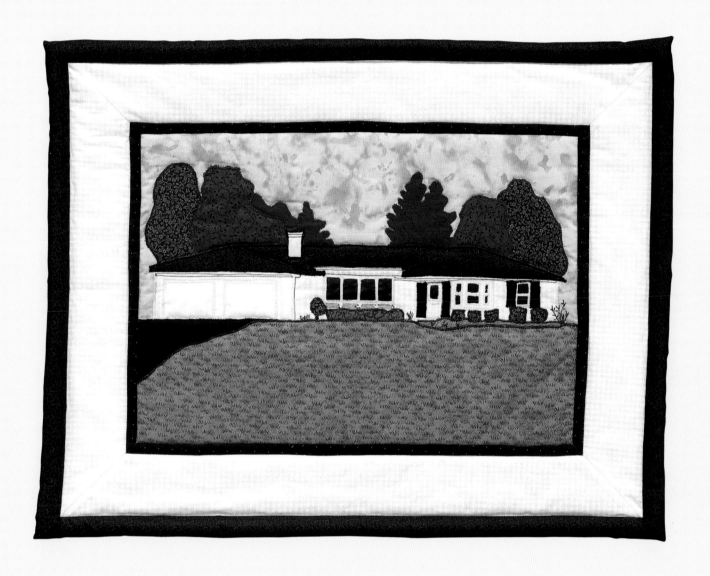

MY HOUSE *by Wendy Rieves, 1995, Brookfield, Wisconsin, 24" x 19".*

THE SUEDBECK HOUSE *by Arlene Suedbeck, 1997, Watertown, Wisconsin, 23" x 19".*
Arlene made this quilt for her son and his family.

THE STRASESKE HOME *by Marian Straseske, 1995, Watertown, Wisconsin, 27" x 21".*

HOUSE FOR SALE *by JoAnn Jacobi, 1995, East Troy, Wisconsin, 29" x 23".*

WINTER CABIN *by Chris Lynn Kirsch, 1993, Sun Prairie, Wisconsin, 14" x 18".*
Jan Weigen had this quilt made for her sons, Jeff and Jay. It depicts their cabin in Hayward, Wisconsin.

THE BROCKWAY HOME *by Barb Brockway, 1995, Oconomowoc, Wisconsin, 23" x 18".*
Barb made this quilt for her son and his family. Note the depth added by Barb's effective repliqué of the home's shadow.

HERMAN AND MATILDA *by Jane Ingersoll, 1997, Sullivan, Wisconsin, 16" x 12".*
These ducks lived in the pond in front of Jane's home. Notice the free-motion machine-embroidered feathers
and the three-dimensional dandelions.

C ABIN IN THE W OODS *by Natalie Sewell, 1994, Madison, Wisconsin, 36" x 27".*
This quilt won a ribbon at the Sun Prairie Quilt Show. Natalie has since become very well known
for her "raw-edge landscape" quilts.

SHADY NOOK *by Kim Knoche, 1994, Madison, Wisconsin, 23" x 17".*
Kim made this as a gift for her father, Herman.
Note the layering of the screened porch and the wonderful hand-embroidered details.

THE KARLS HOME *by Chris Lynn Kirsch, 1993, Sun Prairie, Wisconsin, 38" x 30".*
Hand quilted and owned by Sherry Karls, Waunakee, Wisconsin.
This is a newer structure built to look like a stately old Victorian home. Many parts were salvaged from other structures. The Karlses' attention to detail is wonderful. This project was an exciting repliqué challenge.

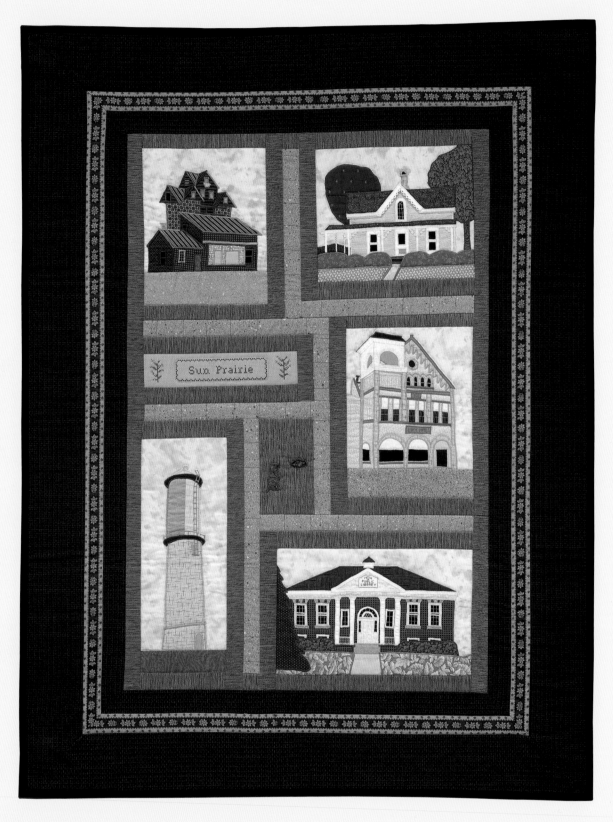

THE SIDEWALKS OF SUN PRAIRIE *by Chris Lynn Kirsch, 1993, Sun Prairie, Wisconsin, 36" x 50".*
This repliqué quilt, one of my earliest, depicts some of the lovely buildings in the city I lived
in at the time. Note the pieced "sidewalks" used to sash the blocks. Jimmy the Groundhog,
our city's mascot, stands near his home in the center of the quilt.

OUTSIDE MY WINDOW *by Chris Lynn Kirsch, 1994, Sun Prairie, Wisconsin, 38″ x 38″.*
I made this quilt as a reminder of the aviary my husband and children made for me at our country home in Sun Prairie, which we had to leave behind due to a job transfer. Note the ever present squirrels and seed hulls in the border.

ROSEDOWN FOUNTAIN *by Wendy Rieves, 2001, Brookfield, Wisconsin, 18" x 17".*
Wendy and Chris led a group of quilters on a Mississippi riverboat cruise in the spring of 2001. This
fountain stands in front of an antebellum mansion they visited, and Wendy chose to save the memory
in a repliqué quilt. Additional foliage was added in a raw-edge appliqué technique, and the water spray
used a combination of glitzy thread, tiny beads, and cheesecloth.

NATCHEZ DOORWAY *by Chris Lynn Kirsch, 2001, Oconomowoc, Wisconsin, 14" x 18".*
The photograph of this door was taken in a unique shop in Natchez, Mississippi.
Note the use of the stained-glass-transom design in the border.

OCONOMOWOC *by Chris Lynn Kirsch, 1998, Oconomowoc, Wisconsin, 24" x 23".*
This quilt was a viewers' choice ribbon winner in a local quilt challenge.

CHAPTER 5

Finishing

This chapter will cover the finishing techniques required to turn the fabric replica into a quilt. Here you will find the basics of adding borders, layering and quilting, and binding the edges of your project. But remember, each project is different, and these are only guidelines to follow. It is up to you to add the special details that make each project unique.

ADDING THE BORDERS

I like to think of repliqué quilts as fabric portraits that will be hung on walls. Therefore a "framed" or "matted" finish that complements the center without overpowering it looks great. It is generally a good idea to pull colors from the quilt's center into the border. Look through the gallery to get ideas for effective borders, but do not limit yourself to these options. Use your imagination. The framing of the antique fire truck with a repliquéd fire hose was the result of a little creative brainstorming (see "Dousman Fire Truck No. 2" on page 48).

I have done many collage quilts that include repliqué blocks. There are numerous options for setting these blocks, from simple sashing to attic windows or even alternating with pieced or appliquéd blocks. This is another opportunity to be imaginative. A collage quilt of the many places a family has called home would make a wonderful gift for parents who "have everything."

Don't eliminate the possibility of using a border fabric or a wide stripe for the border.

These are especially effective when the corners are mitered (see "House for Sale" on page 64 and "The Karls Home" on page 69).

The border strips can also be added with square corners. Instructions for both methods follow. Select the method that best suits your quilt and border fabric.

SQUARE CORNER BORDERS

1. Measure the length of the quilt top through the vertical center. Cut 2 side border strips the length measured and the desired width plus seam allowance. Mark the midpoint of each strip and the quilt sides.

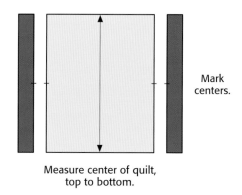

Mark centers.

Measure center of quilt, top to bottom.

2. Pin the border strips to the sides of the quilt top, right sides together, matching midpoints; stitch. Press the seam allowances toward the border strips.

3. Measure the width of the quilt through the horizontal center, including the side borders. Cut the top and bottom border strips the length measured and the desired width

plus seam allowance. Mark the midpoint of each strip and the quilt top and bottom edges.

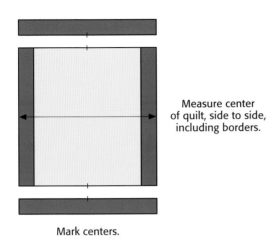

Measure center of quilt, side to side, including borders.

Mark centers.

4. Pin the border strips to the top and bottom edges of the quilt, right sides together, matching midpoints; stitch. Press the seam allowances toward the border strips.

MITERED CORNERS

1. Cut the border strips at least 2" longer than the desired *finished length and width of the quilt*. If you are using a border stripe, before cutting, lay the strip out along the edge of the quilt so that the corners fall at an identical repeat of the design.
2. Mark dots on the back of the quilt top ¼" in from both sides of each corner (4 dots in all, 1 in each corner). Stitch the strips to their respective sides, right sides together, centering the strips on each side and ending the stitching just a thread's width before the dot. Backstitch to secure, leaving the ends of the

border strips loose. Press the seam allowance toward the quilt top.

¼"

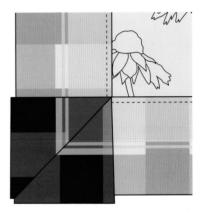

3. Fold the quilt top in half diagonally, right sides together. Align the border strips.
4. Lay the edge of a 24"-long quilting ruler along the quilt fold with the 45° line along the border seam.
5. Draw a line on the wrong side of the border strip from the corner mark to the border strip outside edge.

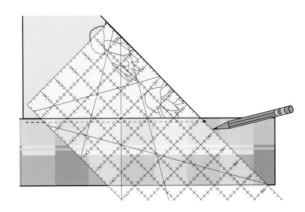

6. Pin along the marked line. Stitch along the marked line, beginning a thread's width from the point where the border seams meet.

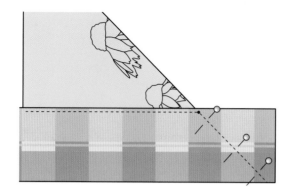

7. Check the miter from the right side, and when you are sure it lies flat, press all border seams toward the borders. Trim the miters and press them to one side.

> *Tip* If the miter is puckered, it is most likely because the three seams are touching or even overlapping each other. If you stop a thread's width away, puckering should be eliminated.

REMOVING THE PAPER

Once the quilt has been bordered, the paper must be removed from the back of the piece. Most of the paper should tear away quite easily due to the many perforations made while stitching, but pull away very carefully wherever straight stitching was used to create an effect, such as windowpane lines and railings. If you have difficulty removing any pieces, try using a pair of tweezers with pointed ends.

LAYERING AND BASTING THE QUILT SANDWICH

After the paper has been removed, the quilt top is ready for layering with batting and backing.

1. Cut a piece of backing fabric and a piece of thin, flat quilt batting 1" larger than the quilt top all around.
2. Lay the backing, wrong side up, on the work surface. Secure it with masking tape in several places along the edges to keep it smooth and taut.
3. Smooth the batting over the backing, and then center the quilt top over the batting, right side up.
4. Baste the layers together, using safety pins placed approximately every 3" (I prefer size 1 safety pins).

QUILTING

Repliqué quilts require very simple quilting so that the picture itself is the central focus. I tend to machine quilt, rather than quilt by hand, because the nature of the repliqué technique creates areas with many layers of fabric. This added thickness makes hand quilting difficult.

On quilts featuring buildings, straight stitching with a walking foot around the main architectural details will hold things together. Free-motion stitching around curved items works well, and if there is a large expanse of sky, adding clouds with stitches can be very effective. Quilting can also be used to create lines for siding or shingles if you have used a solid fabric.

Quilts that feature images other than building, like the scissors and purple coneflowers, also require only stitching around the main objects. Because these blocks often have many curves, free-motion stitching is again a good choice.

ADDING A HANGING SLEEVE

To continue the portrait look, add a sleeve to the back of the quilt so the method of hanging does not show from the front. A thin (1/4") wooden dowel slides easily into the sleeve to hang the quilt and give it even support. For a small quilt, rest the dowel on one center nail. On a larger quilt, use a nail at each end of the dowel plus the one in the center. The center nail eliminates sagging.

1. Cut a strip of fabric 3" wide and the length of the quilt upper edge minus 1".
2. Cut the strip in half widthwise. Turn under 1/4" along each short end and machine stitch in place.
3. Trim the batting and backing even with the quilt top, making sure the corners are square. Pin through all 3 layers along the outer edge at 2" intervals.
4. Fold the sleeve strips in half lengthwise, wrong sides together. Align the long raw edges with the top edge of the quilt, leaving 1/2" between the 2 sleeves. Pin the sleeve strips in place.

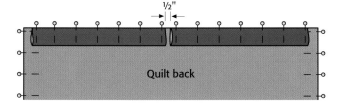

Quilt back

5. Bind the quilt as described in "Binding" (below). After the top edges of the sleeves have been caught in the binding, hand stitch the lower edge of the sleeve strips to the back of the quilt. Be sure the stitches do not go through to the quilt front.

BINDING

There are many, many ways to bind a quilt, and I think I have tried them all. The following method is a combination of my favorite techniques. I have found it to give a wonderful finished edge to the quilt.

1. To determine binding-strip width, multiply the finished binding width (I like 1/2" for repliqué wall quilts) by 4. Cut enough strips of binding fabric to go around the outside of the quilt, plus at least 10" to allow for turning corners and joining strips together. Join the strips with diagonal seams into 1 long strip.

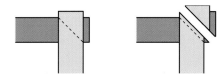

2. To find where to begin, lay the binding around the outside edge of the quilt, and arrange the binding so that no seams fall at the quilt corners. When you are satisfied with the placement, lay the beginning of the binding strip on the quilt top, right sides together, with the binding raw edge aligned with the quilt top raw edge.
3. Use a 1/2" seam allowance and a walking foot to stitch the binding to the quilt top. Begin by backstitching 8" from the beginning of the strip and stop 1/2" from the corner; backstitch and remove the quilt from the machine.

4. With the corner facing you, fold the binding up to create a 45° angle. Fold the binding down over the angled fold, creating another fold that is even with the upper edge. The raw edges of the binding should be even with the next side.

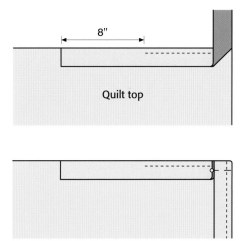

5. Begin stitching at the edge of the quilt and stitch until you are ½" from the next corner. Repeat step 4. Repeat for all 4 corners, stopping 8" from where you originally began stitching.

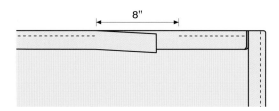

6. Cut the end tail only at a 45° angle, halfway between the beginning and ending stitching.

7. Lay the end tail over the beginning tail and draw the angle on the beginning tail.

8. Lift up the end tail and cut the beginning tail ½" beyond the drawn line, toward the end of the strip.

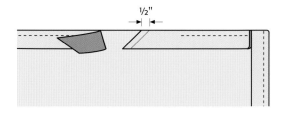

9. Lift the binding off the quilt and place the ends right sides together as shown. Stitch the ends together using a ¼" seam allowance.

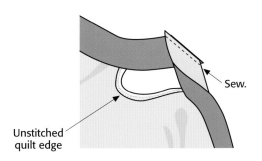

10. Lay the binding back on the quilt with the raw edges aligned. Beginning where you stopped, stitch the unstitched portion of the binding to the quilt top, backstitching at the beginning and end.

11. Turn the binding to the back of the quilt. Fold the binding raw edge to meet the quilt raw edge. The fold created should be ½" from the quilt edge. Now fold at the quilt edge so the binding just covers the binding seam on the back.

12. Secure the binding with pins or binding clips and hand stitch the binding to the back of the quilt, mitering the corners.

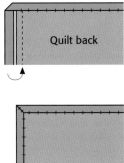

MAKING A LABEL

Making a label is the last step, but I feel it is one of the most important. A quilt may be lovely to look at, but its value increases tremendously when its story is told. Because most repliqué quilts are made from a photograph, I think it is a great idea to have the photograph somewhere on the quilt. The following are my two favorite labeling methods.

PHOTO LABEL

We live in a wonderful era, when pictures can be printed directly onto fabric. My favorite product for making these labels is June Tailor's Colorfast Printer Fabric. It is a premium cotton muslin that has been backed with paper so it feeds through regular ink-jet printers. The fabric has been treated so that the ink becomes permanent on the fabric. To make a photo label I scan my photo into my computer, add the quilt's name, my name, the place it was made, the year and any other pertinent information (in a font much nicer than my penmanship) and print it onto the Colorfast Printer Fabric

following the package instructions. The label is then ready to appliqué to the back of the quilt. You can also use photo-transfer products.

PHOTO POCKET LABEL

Another lovely way to add the picture to the label is by attaching a vinyl pocket.

1. Cut a piece of muslin 1" larger than the size of the snapshot for the label. Design the label either by hand or computer, and remember to include all of the important information about the quilt and quilter. Appliqué the label to the back of the quilt.

2. Cut a piece of clear, non-adhesive vinyl 1" larger than the snapshot. Cover the edges of the vinyl with double-fold bias tape and stitch it in place using a zipper foot or Teflon-coated foot (a regular foot tends to stick to the vinyl).

3. Appliqué the vinyl pocket over the label along the bottom and sides. Slide the photograph into the pocket.

About the Author

Chris Lynn Kirsch learned to sew as a child and was taking tailoring classes by her senior year of high school, but she didn't discover quiltmaking until she was married and had children. She graduated from college as a dental hygienist but is dedicated to quilting full time now. Chris loves quilting, a vocation she has been able to adjust to fit the schedules of her husband, Michael, and two children, Heather and Brad.

Chris found her passion for quilting when her sister-in-law, Mary Sue, talked her into taking a class. She began making every pattern she could find and creating techniques and designs when she couldn't find the patterns she wanted. She has no background in art, so finding that she could design was a wonderful discovery. Chris currently teaches quilting at two technical colleges, at quilt shows, and for guilds and shops. She loves to take challenges and enter competitions. Chris's quilts have won ribbons and been displayed nationally and in Europe.